Management
Th
Accounting

cial terminology of the CIMA

The Chartered Institute of Management Accountants
Portland Place
London W1N 4AB

D0275885

Reprinted (with ammendments) January 1984
Reprinted September 1984
Reprinted June 1987
Reprinted October 1988
Reprinted May 1989
Reprinted October 1989
ISBN 0 901308 67 6

CONTENTS

LIST OF ILLUSTRATIONS

FOREWORD

This terminology is issued by authority of the Council of the Institute and is the fourth major revision of the original terminology published in 1937.

The objective is to encourage the orderly use of management accounting terms and to achieve a better understanding between accountants and management, and indeed between one accountant and another, in the belief that this should lead to advancement in the proficiency of professional management as a whole. The reader is urged to use the official terms wherever possible.

Accounting is essentially evolutionary, hence the need for updating its terminology. Its restatement at a point in time is not intended to be restrictive but to provide a pause for consolidating practical and examination usage as a platform for further evolution.

The Institute thanks the members who directly compiled this terminology, Douglas Mayman FCMA FCCA JDipMA (Chairman of the Working Party), Brian Bishop FCMA JDipMA FCIS (An Institute Medallist), Derek Holford FCMA, and members of the Institute staff, Bernard Cox FCMA FCCA, John Keen FCMA and Alex Young FCMA BCom PhD FCA JDipMA; also members of the Research and Technical Committee and many other members for their helpful comments. The British Standards Institution is thanked for permission to use a number of definitions in sections 3 and 11.

President
December 1982

INTRODUCTION

Scope
Management accountancy covers several fields, and this terminology is intended to provide an overview of the terms relating to them. Specialist fields such as mathematics, economics, statistics, law and taxation have their own language, and only brief reference can be made to them in a work of this nature. In such cases the terminology is not intended to be exhaustive but to provide an insight which should lead to further enquiry.

Implementation
The terminology will enable accountants to communicate more effectively, and it is suggested that they adopt the terms in accounting manuals, in common usage and in training schemes for students. Members of the Institute are expected to implement it in this way. This terminology will be adopted by the Institute as the basis for examinations. In using it, students will know that they are following the best professional practice and that an increasing number of examination boards will accept it as a common standard.

Relevant definitions are included from, or based on, Statements of Standard Accounting Practice and the Companies Acts 1948 to 1981. These definitions supersede terms used in many existing textbooks. The reference *the Companies Act* is used in the terminology as an abbreviation for those definitions which are derived from the 8th schedule to the Companies Act 1948, which itself was introduced by the Companies Act 1981.

No responsibility for loss occasioned to any person acting or refraining from action as a result of any material in this publication can be accepted by the authors or publishers.

International practice
While this terminology is in English and is therefore applicable to most English speaking countries, each of these has a minority of synonymous terms and a different usage of the same term. Possibly the best known of these is the American use of the word *burden* meaning overhead. A comprehensive list of these national variations has not been attempted since they do not invalidate the basic definitions which follow United Kingdom practice.

Reference
The terms have been classified into twelve sections, as shown on the contents page, and are listed alphabetically within each section. For ease of reference the terms are indexed at the back of the book. Illustrations are given where it is considered that they will assist further understanding of a principle or application.

Section I

ACCOUNTING CONCEPTS AND TERMS

account

A structured record of monetary transactions, kept as part of an accounting system.

This may be a simple list, or entries on a debit and credit basis, in either visible form or in a computer processed form, such as on a magnetic tape or disc. *See* figure 1.1 for an illustration of the relationship of accounts.

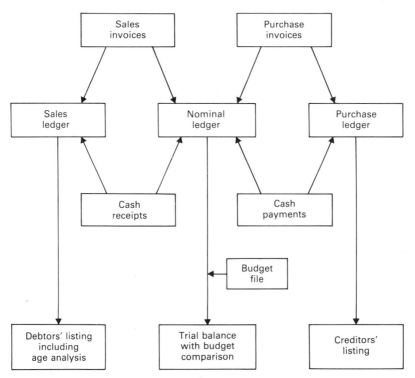

Note: The Nominal ledger contains the cash account

Figure 1.1 Relationship of accounts

accountancy
The profession whose members practise accounting.

accountant
A member of the profession which practises accounting.

accounting
1. The classification and recording of actual transactions in monetary terms, and
2. the presentation and interpretation of the results of those transactions in order to assess performance over a period, and the financial position at a given date, and
3. the projection in monetary terms of future activities arising from alternative planned courses of action. *See* figure 1.2.

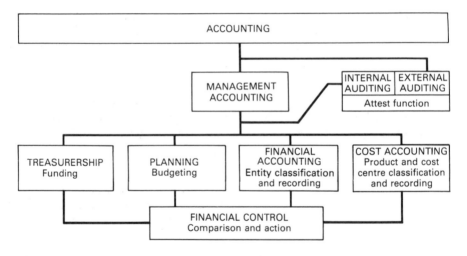

Figure 1.2   Accounting: functional relationships

accounting bases
The methods developed for applying fundamental accounting concepts to financial transactions and items, for the purpose of financial accounts, and in particular (a) for determining the accounting periods in which revenue and costs should be recognised in the profit and loss account and (b) for determining the amounts at which material items should be stated in the balance sheet (SSAP 2).

accounting instructions
Instructions on the way the accounting system is to be operated by staff.
Note: The use of the term *standing instructions* for this purpose is not recommended.

accounting manual(s)
A collection of accounting instructions governing the responsibilities of persons, and the procedures, forms and records relating to the preparation and use of accounting data.
There can thus be separate manuals for the constituent parts of accounting, e.g. *budget manual, cost accounting manual.*

accounting period
The period of time covered by the accounting statements of an entity.
There may be different time periods for different accounting statements, e.g. cost accounts may be for four or five week periods to coincide with a thirteen week financial accounting period. The term *fiscal year* is used in the USA to mean an accounting period of one year. In the UK however fiscal year is generally understood to mean tax year.

accounting policies
The specific accounting bases selected and consistently followed by a business enterprise as being, in the opinion of the management, appropriate to its circumstances and best suited to present fairly its results and financial position (SSAP 2).

adjusting events
Post balance sheet events which provide additional evidence of conditions existing at the balance sheet date; they include events which because of statutory or conventional requirements are reflected in financial statements (SSAP 17).
Note: An adjusting event, where material, means that changes should be made in the financial statements up to the balance sheet date.

amortisation
The provision for the using up of a wasting asset, e.g. oil fields, mines or quarries or of a fixed asset which has a predetermined useful life, e.g. leases or intangible assets. *See also* depreciation.

audit
A systematic examination of the activities and status of an entity based primarily on investigation and analysis of its systems, controls and records. *See* external audit, internal audit and management audit.

audit: external
A periodic examination of the books of account and records of an entity carried out by an independent third party (the auditor), to ensure that they have been properly maintained, are accurate and comply with established concepts, principles, accounting standards, legal requirements and give a true and fair view of the financial state of the entity.

audit: internal
An independent appraisal activity established within an organisation as a service to it. It is a control which functions by examining and evaluating the adequacy and effectiveness of other controls.

Originally concerned with the financial records, the investigative techniques developed are now applied to the analysis of the effectiveness of all parts of an entity's operations and management. *See also* management audit.

auditing standards
Those Statements of Auditing Standards which are approved for issue by the Councils of the UK accountancy bodies listed in the Explanatory Foreword of the standards, and which are effective for the period covered by the financial statements on which the auditor is reporting.

balance (on an account)
The difference between the totals of the debit and credit entries in an account.

book-keeping
That part of accounting which deals with the recording of actual transactions in monetary terms.

This may be in books, or on cards, tape or disc, or a combination of these.

capital gain (loss)
The extent by which the net realised value of a capital asset exceeds (or in the case of a capital loss is less than) the cost of acquisition plus additional improvements, less depreciation charges where applicable.

It can also arise from the exchange of such an asset for another of a different type. The term can have different interpretations for tax purposes depending upon current legislation.

capital surplus
The surplus distributed amongst shareholders in accordance with their rights under the articles of association after the discharge of all outstanding costs and liabilities following the liquidation of a company.

cash flow
The cash generated or spent in a given period. *See* figure 10.1.

classification
The arrangement of items in logical groups having regard to their nature (subjective classification) or the purpose to be fulfilled (objective classification). *See* next item.

code
A system of symbols designed to be applied to a classified set of items, to give a brief accurate reference facilitating entry, collation and analysis.

For example, in costing systems, composite symbols are commonly used. In the composite symbol 211.392 the first three digits might indicate the nature of the expenditure (subjective classification), while the last three digits might indicate the cost centre or cost unit to be charged (objective classification). *See also* nominal account, page 107.

concept: accrual/matching
The concept that revenues and costs are matched one with the other and dealt with in the profit and loss account of the period to which they relate irrespective of the period of receipt or payment (SSAP 2). To accrue an amount is to post it to the accounts in accordance with the matching concept.

concept: consistency
The principle that there is a consistency of treatment of like items (accounting bases and policies) within each accounting period and from one period to the next (SSAP 2).

concept: fundamental accounting
The basic assumptions which underlie the periodic financial accounts of business enterprises, and may affect the way in which accounting information is collected, processed and disseminated.

concept: going concern
The assumption that the enterprise will continue in operational existence for the forseeable future (SSAP 2).

concept: lower of cost or net realisable value
A concept of stock valuation whereby goods in stock are valued at actual or standard cost, or at replacement cost or net realisable value whichever is lower.

concept: materiality
The principle that financial statements should separately disclose items which are significant enough to affect evaluation or decisions. (*cont.*)

The level of significance is a matter for individual judgement. Thus an entity may decide to treat all fixed assets which cost less than, say, £500 as revenue expenditure because the amounts are not *material* to the entity's financial results. Materiality may be considered in the context of the financial statements as a whole, the balance sheet, the profit and loss account, or individual items within the financial statements. In addition, depending upon the nature of the matter, materiality may be considered in relative or absolute terms.

concept: money measurement

The concept that financial accounting information relates only to those activities which can be expressed in monetary terms.

concept: prudence

The concept that revenue and profits are not anticipated, but are recognised by inclusion in the profit and loss account only when realised in the form either of cash or of other assets the ultimate cash realisation of which can be assessed with reasonable certainty; provision is made for all known liabilities (expenses and losses) whether the amount of these is known with certainty or is a best estimate in the light of the information available (SSAP 2).

concept: realisation

The concept that profit is only accounted for when it is realised and not when it can be recognised.

contra

A book-keeping term meaning against, or on the opposite side.

It is usually used where debits are matched with related credits, in the same or a different account. (A common example is where a supplier is also a customer).

cost

1 (as a noun). The amount of expenditure (actual or notional) incurred on, or attributable to, a specified thing or activity.

2 (as a verb). To ascertain the cost of a specified thing or activity.

Note: The word *cost* can rarely stand alone and should be qualified as to its nature and limitations.

cost accounting

That part of management accounting which establishes budgets and standard costs and actual costs of operations, processes, departments or products and the analysis of variances, profitability or social use of funds.

The use of the term *costing* is not recommended.

cost audit
The verification of cost records and accounts and a check on the adherence to the prescribed cost accounting procedures and the continuing relevance of such procedures.

cost of sales adjustment (COSA)
The difference between the current value to the business of stock consumed at the time of consumption and the cost of stock charged on an historical cost basis.

The resulting total charge thus represents the value to the business of stock consumed in earning the revenue of the period (SSAP 16).

current cost
The calculated cost of acquiring goods for processing or resale, or of assets, at the time when their value is consumed by the entity, usually obtained by some form of averaging or index.

current cost accounting (CCA)
A system of accounting based upon a concept of capital which is represented by the net operating assets of a business.

These net operating assets (fixed assets, stocks and monetary working capital) are the same as those included in historical cost accounts, but in the current cost accounts the fixed assets and stock are normally expressed at current price levels. The objective of current cost accounts is to provide guidance for management, shareholders and others on such matters as the financial viability of the business and distribution decisions (SSAP 16).

Note: SSAP 16 requires that the charges to the profit and loss account are based on the value of assets to the business at the date of consumption and balance sheet values of non-monetary assets are stated at their value to the business at the balance sheet date. For UK entities four adjustments are required to historical profit and loss accounts. They are the depreciation adjustment, cost of sales adjustment (COSA), monetary working capital adjustment (MWCA), and a gearing adjustment. In the balance sheet, the change from historical to current values is reflected in the current cost reserve.

current purchasing power accounting (CPP)
A system of accounting for inflation in which the values of the non-monetary items in the historical cost accounting statements are adjusted to reflect changes in the general purchasing power of money.

Adjustments are made using a general price index.

double entry book-keeping
The most commonly used system of book-keeping on visible or non-visible records based on the principle that every financial transaction involves the simultaneous receiving and giving of value by two entities.

The former is debited and the latter is credited. At the end of a period the value of all debits posted equals the value of all credits posted. Double entry book-keeping is sometimes referred to as double entry accounting.

equity method of accounting
A method of accounting under which the investment in a company is shown in the consolidated balance sheet at:
(a) the cost of the investment; and
(b) the investing company or group's share of the post-acquisition retained profits and reserves of the company; less
(c) any amounts written off in respect of (a) and (b) above;
and under which the investing company accounts separately in its profit and loss account for its share of the profits before tax, taxation and extraordinary items of the company concerned (SSAP 14).

financial accounting
That part of accounting which covers the classification and recording of actual transactions of an entity in monetary terms in accordance with established concepts, principles, accounting standards and legal requirements and presents as accurate a view as possible of the effect of those transactions over a period of time and at the end of that time.

financial/cost accounts calendar adjustment
A self-balancing adjustment of financial and cost accounts to align the results shown in them when expenses are charged in financial accounts according to calendar time but in cost accounts according to working days.

A simple example is property rates, where the charge in a 13 week quarter's financial accounts would be one quarter of the total year's rates, regardless of the fact that there may be two weeks' factory holiday in that period: in this case the charge in the cost accounts could be 11/48 of the total year. These differences can be accommodated by various methods, the most commonly used being:
1. using the calculated differences as reconciling factors,
2. adjusting cost accounts to financial accounts,

Overhead cost		Year	Month 1	2	3	4	5	6	7	8	9	10	11	12
	Calendar weeks	52	4	4	5	4	4	5	4	4	5	4	4	5
	Working days	240	18	20	25	18	19	25	10	20	25	20	20	20
Salaries	£2,000 week	104,000	8,000	8,000	10,000	8,000	8,000	10,000	8,000	8,000	10,000	8,000	8,000	10,000
Rates	£1,000 week	52,000	4,000	4,000	5,000	4,000	4,000	5,000	4,000	4,000	5,000	4,000	4,000	5,000
Electricity	Max demand £20 week	1,040	80	80	100	80	80	100	80	80	100	80	80	100
	Units seasonally	4,800	550	500	450	400	300	200	200	300	400	450	500	550
Heating oil	Heating periods only	1,500	250	200	200	100	—	—	—	—	100	200	200	250
Indirect wages	£200 per working day	48,000	3,600	4,000	5,000	3,600	3,800	5,000	2,000	4,000	5,000	4,000	4,000	4,000
Total overheads as fin. a/cs		211,340	16,480	16,780	20,750	16,180	16,180	20,300	14,280	16,380	20,600	16,730	16,780	19,900
Budgeted absorption in cost accounts (rounded = £880 per working day)		211,340	15,849	17,612	22,015	15,849	16,731	22,015	8,806	17,612	22,015	17,612	17,612	17,612
Calendar adj.	P & L a/c	—	-631	+832	+1,265	-331	+551	+1,715	-5,474	+1,232	+1,415	+882	+832	-2,288
Cumulative	Bal. sheet	—	-631	+201	+1,466	+1,135	+1,686	+3,401	-2,073	-841	+574	+1,456	+2,288	—

Figure 1.3 Calendar adjustment calculation

3. adjusting financial accounts to cost accounts by prepaying or accruing one total figure for all cost category differences. *See* figure 1.3 for example.

historical cost
The actual cost of acquiring assets, or goods and services.

historical cost accounting
A system of accounting in which all values (in revenue and capital accounts) are based on the costs actually incurred or as revalued from time to time.

imprest system
A method of controlling cash or stock: when the cash or stock has been reduced by disbursements it is restored to its original level: at all times the cash or stock in hand plus the value of issues has a fixed value.

incomplete records
A term used to signify any accounting system which does not in its entirety conform to double entry accounting.
Varying degrees of incompleteness can occur.

integrated accounts
A set of accounting records which provides financial and cost accounts using a common input of data for all accounting purposes.

interlocking accounts
A system in which the cost accounts are distinct from the financial accounts, the two sets of accounts being kept continuously in agreement by the use of control accounts or made readily reconcilable by other means.

management accounting
The provision of information required by management for such purposes as:
1. formulation of policies,
2. planning and controlling the activities of the enterprise,
3. decision taking on alternative courses of action,
4. disclosure to those external to the entity (shareholders and others),
5. disclosure to employees,
6. safeguarding assets.
The above involves participation in management to ensure that there is effective:
(a) formulation of plans to meet objectives (long term planning),
(b) formulation of short term operation plans (budgeting/profit planning),

(c) recording of actual transactions (financial accounting and cost accounting),
(d) corrective action to bring future actual transactions into line (financial control),
(e) obtaining and controlling finance (treasurership). *See* figure 1.4,
(f) reviewing and reporting on systems and operations (internal audit, management audit).
See figure 1.2.

management accounting guidelines
Statements of good management accounting practice which are advisory not mandatory issued by companies and professional accountancy bodies and in particular by the Institute of Cost and Management Accountants.

net realisable value
The price at which goods in stock could be currently sold less any further costs which would be incurred to complete the sale.

non-adjusting events
Post balance sheet events which concern conditions which did not exist at the balance sheet date (SSAP 17).
Note: Where non-adjusting events are material, disclosure is required if non-disclosure would affect the ability of the users of financial statements to reach a proper understanding of the financial position.

off balance sheet finance
Sources of finance which do not appear on the balance sheet; generally, the use of assets which are not owned.
A common example in the past has been finance leasing.

post balance sheet events
Those events, both favourable and unfavourable, which occur between the balance sheet date and the date on which the financial statements are approved by the board of directors, or equivalent in other organisations.
They are classified into adjusting events and non-adjusting events, *q.v.* (SSAP 17).

real account
A record of transactions relating to a tangible asset.

reconciled accounts
A system in which monetary transactions are processed independently through financial accounts and cost accounts, the results of those

transactions then being compared and reasons for differences accounted for and explained.

replacement cost accounting
(i) A family of techniques which seeks to show whether or not the value of physical assets of the business has been maintained in financial terms.
(ii) Methods of accounting which include among others:
(a) showing freehold and leasehold property at current market values,
(b) showing all fixed assets and depreciation at current replacement values in their present age and condition and for similar use,
(c) showing fixed assets and stock, with depreciation and cost of sales, at current replacement values,
(d) as in (c), with the equity interest adjusted for the general price level change, and with monetary assets and liabilities at their original money values, with consequential adjustments to profit.

responsibility accounting
A system of accounting that segregates revenues and costs into areas of personal responsibility in order to assess the performance attained by persons to whom authority has been assigned. *See also* budgetary control.

single entry book-keeping
A form of incomplete records book-keeping in which the dual aspect of transactions is not explicit and in which usually the cash book is the only record kept.

standard accounting practice
A definitive standard of financial accounting and reporting set out in a Statement of Standard Accounting Practice (SSAP) encompassing:
(a) fundamentals of financial accounting,
(b) definition of terms used,
(c) application of fundamentals to specific classes of business,
(d) the form and content of financial statements including presentation and disclosure.
(*Source:* UK Accounting Standards Committee)

treasurership
The function concerned with the provision and use of finance as distinct from the control function.
Treasurership includes provision of capital, short term borrowing, foreign currency management, banking, collections, money market

investment and (sometimes) insurance. The distinction between the treasury and control functions is illustrated in figure 1.4.

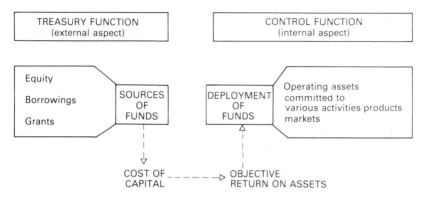

Figure 1.4   Relationship of the treasury and control functions

uniform accounting

A common system using agreed concepts, principles and standard accounting practice adopted by different entities in the same industry to ensure that they all deal with accounting information in a like manner, the objective being to facilitate interfirm comparison.

value added

The increase in realisable value resulting from an alteration in form, location or availability of a product or service, excluding the cost of purchased materials and services.

Note: Unlike conversion cost, value added includes profit.

Section 2

ORGANISATIONS AND COMMERCIAL CONCEPTS

articles of association

The document which, with the memorandum of association, provides the legal constitution of a company.

The articles of association define the rules and regulations governing the management of its affairs, the rights of members of the company, and the duties and powers of the directors.

associated company

A company not being a subsidiary of the investing group or company in which:

(a) the interest of the investing group or company is effectively that of a partner in a joint venture or consortium and the investing group or company is in a position to exercise a significant influence over the company in which the investment is made; or

(b) the interest of the investing group or company is for the long term, and is substantial and, having regard to the disposition of the other shareholdings, the investing group or company is in a position to exercise a significant influence over the company in which the investment is made (SSAP 1 Revised).

bankruptcy

The legal status of an individual against whom an adjudication order has been made by the court primarily because of his inability to meet his financial liabilities.

beta factor

The measure of a share's relative volatility in terms of market risk.

If a specific stock market share indicator moves up or down by 10 per cent and share X rises or falls by 20 per cent in the same direction, then share X is twice as volatile as the average share in that sector and is assigned a beta factor of two.

budget centre

A section of an organisation for which separate budgets can be prepared and control exercised.

chartered entity
An organisation formed by the grant of a royal charter by the crown. The charter authorises the entity to operate and states the powers specifically granted.

Examples: Bank of England, Hudson's Bay Company, The Institute of Cost and Management Accountants.

company/corporation
A legal entity, the life of which is independent of that of its members.

There are three ways of forming a company or corporation, namely by charter, by Act of Parliament or by registration under the Companies Acts.

company limited by guarantee
A company in which each member undertakes, on a winding-up, to contribute (to the limit of his guarantee) towards the payment of the liabilities of the company.

The Companies Act 1980 stipulates that no new registrations of this nature will be made.

company limited by shares/joint stock company/limited liability company
A company in which the liability of members for the company's debts is limited to the amount, if any, unpaid on the shares taken up by them.

concept: business entity
The concept that financial accounting information relates only to the activities of the business entity and not to the activities of its owner(s).

conglomerate
An entity comprising a number of dissimilar businesses.

consortium
An association of several entities with a view to carrying out a joint activity.

Note: A separate organisation may, or may not, be created for the management of the activity.

contribution centre
A profit centre where expenditure is calculated on a marginal cost basis.

cost centre
A location, function or items of equipment in respect of which costs may be ascertained and related to cost units for control purposes.

debt capacity
The extent to which an entity can raise loan finance.

debt factoring
The sale of debts to a third party (the factor) at a discount, in return for prompt cash.

The most usual arrangement is that A notifies B on the face of its invoice that the debt has been assigned to the factor, to whom payment should be made. A factoring service may be *with recourse*, in which case A takes the risk of the debt not being eventually paid by B, or *without recourse* when the factor takes the risk. The term is often used in its shortened form of *factoring*.

entity
An economic unit that has a separate, distinct identity, e.g. industrial and commercial companies, charities, local authorities, government agencies.

finance lease
A lease that transfers substantially all the risks and rewards of ownership of an asset to the lessee.

It should be presumed that such a transfer of risks and rewards occurs if at the start of a lease the present value of the minimum lease payments, including any initial payment, amounts to substantially all (normally 90 per cent or more) of the fair value of the leased asset to the lessor at the start of the lease. The present value should be calculated by using the rate of interest implicit in the lease, or if this is not practical, a commercial rate of interest.

Note: Finance leases are for the major part of an asset's life, and the owner (the lessor) expects to get his normal profit on the asset without being involved in further activity. The lessee is responsible for repairs, maintenance and insurance. The lessor's involvement is purely one of financing. 'Fair value' above is the price at which an asset could be exchanged in an arm's length transaction less, where applicable, any grants receivable towards the purchase or use of the asset.

group
A holding company and its subsidiaries (SSAP 1).

hire purchase
A contract for the hire of an asset which contains a provision giving the hirer an option to acquire legal title to the asset upon the fulfilment of certain conditions stated in the contract.

holding company

A company is a holding company of another if, but only if, that other is its subsidiary as defined. *See* subsidiary company.

insolvency

The inability of a debtor to pay his debts as and when they fall due.

investment centre

A profit centre in which inputs are measured in terms of expenses and outputs are measured in terms of revenues, and in which assets employed are also measured, the excess of revenue over expenditure then being related to assets employed.

joint venture

A project undertaken by two or more persons/entities joining together with a view to profit, normally in connection with a single operation.

lease

A contract between a lessor and a lessee for the hire of a specific asset.

The lessor retains ownership of the asset but conveys the right to the use of the asset to the lessee for an agreed period of time in return for the payment of specified rentals. There are two kinds of lease, the finance lease and the operating lease.

liquidation

The winding up of a company, in which the assets are sold, liabilities settled as far as possible, and any remaining cash is returned to the owners. *See also* voluntary liquidation.

mark-down

A term used in retailing, wholesaling and factoring for a reduction in selling price for reasons of damage or slow sales.

mark-up

A term used in retailing, wholesaling and factoring to indicate the addition to the cost price of goods to produce a required selling price, often expressed as a percentage.

market risk premium

The extra return required from a share to compensate for its risk compared with the average risk of the market.

memorandum of association

The document which, with the articles of association, provides the legal constitution of a company.

The memorandum states the name and registered office of the company. It also defines its powers and objects and usually states that the liability of its members is limited.

merger
The amalgamation of two or more separate entities.

A merger of companies or corporations may be brought about by an exchange of shares or the creation of a new entity.

nominee holding
A shareholding in a company registered in the name of a nominee, instead of that of the owner.

offer for sale
An advertisement containing a prospectus offering new shares for sale of a company which is already quoted on a stock exchange.

operating lease
A lease other than a finance lease.

Note: The risks and benefits of ownership are usually the responsibility of the lessor. He is usually responsible for repairs, maintenance and insurance. He carries the risk of obsolescence and the residual value at the end of the lease is important to him.

over/under capitalisation
Terms used to describe a surplus or deficiency of permanent capital in relation to the current level of activity of a business.

overtrading
A term applied to a business which enters into commitments in excess of its available short-term liquid resources.

This can arise due to a time lag even if the company is trading profitably, e.g. the effect of a long production cycle. *Note:* It is illegal to continue trading when having reasonable grounds to believe liabilities to creditors cannot be met.

See also voluntary liquidation.

partnership
The relationship which exists between persons carrying on business in common with a view to profit (Partnership Act 1890 or Limited Partnership Act 1907).

The liability of the individual partners is unlimited, unless the partnership agreement provides for any limitation. A partnership consists of not more than twenty persons, except in certain cases, e.g. practising solicitors, professional accountants and members of the Stock Exchange, where this figure may be exceeded.

private company
Unless the Companies Acts otherwise require, a private company is a company that is not a public company. It must have at least two members (Companies Act 1980).

A private company must include as the last part of its name the word *limited* or the abbreviation *ltd* (Companies Act 1948).

production cost centre
A cost centre in which production is carried on: this may embrace one specific operation, e.g. machining, or a continuous process, e.g. distillation.

profit centre
A segment of the business entity by which both revenues are received and expenditures are caused or controlled, such revenues and expenditure being used to evaluate segmental performance.

This may also be called a *business centre*, *business unit*, or *strategic business unit*, depending upon the concept of management responsibility prevailing in the entity concerned.

prospectus
An invitation to the public to apply for the shares or debentures of a company.

public limited company (p.l.c. or Welsh equivalent c.c.c.)
A company limited by shares or limited by guarantee and having a share capital, being a company:
(a) the memorandum of which states that the company is to be a public limited company; and
(b) in relation to which the provisions of the Companies Acts as to the registration or re-registration of a company as a public limited company have been complied with on or after the appointed day (22nd December, 1980); and
(c) which has at least two members.

A public limited company is required to include as the last part of its name the words *public limited company* or Welsh equivalent or the letters *p.l.c.* or, in Wales, the letters *c.c.c.* (Companies Act 1980).

redemption
Repayment, this term being most frequently used in connection with preference shares and debentures.

register of directors' shareholdings
A record kept by a company showing the number of issued shares in that company held by each of its directors.

registered company

A company incorporated under the Companies Acts.

It is a body corporate having perpetual succession and a common seal. The liability of its members to contribute to the assets of the company in the event of its being wound up are determined by the Acts.

responsibility centre

A unit or function of an organisation headed by a manager having direct responsibility for its performance.

revenue centre

A centre devoted to raising revenue with no responsibility for production, e.g. a sales centre, often used in a not-for-profit organisation.

service cost centre

A cost centre for the provision of a service or services to other cost centres.

Note: When the output of an organisation is a service, rather than goods, it is usual to use some alternative term such as *support cost centre* or *utility cost centre* for supporting services.

share register

A record kept by a company of the ownership of its issued shares.

In public limited companies such registers are updated frequently as share ownership changes, usually on computer files, and cut off dates are used for dividend payments.

sole trader

A person carrying on business with sole legal responsibility for its actions, not in partnership nor as a company.

statutory body

An entity formed by Act of Parliament.

The Act defines the powers of the statutory body and authorises its operations. This method of company formation is confined normally to the nationalised industries such as the National Coal Board and public undertakings such as the Independent Broadcasting Authority. From 1974 newly formed authorities administering the system of local government owe their existence to the Local Government Act 1972.

subsidiary company

A company shall be deemed to be a subsidiary of another if, but only if
(a) that other either:
(i) is a member of it and controls the composition of its Board of Directors, or
(ii) holds more than half in nominal value of its equity share capital, or
(b) the first mentioned company is a subsidiary of any company which is that other's subsidiary,
and it otherwise comes within the terms of Section 154 of the Companies Act 1948 (SSAP14).

take-over/acquisition

The acquiring, by one business, of a controlling interest in the voting share capital or the assets of another. *See also* holding company and subsidiary company.

voluntary liquidation

The winding up of a limited company by resolution of the company itself, which may either be
(a) a members' voluntary winding up with a statutory declaration as to the ability to pay all debts in full, or
(b) a creditors' voluntary winding up when the liquidator is under the control of the creditors.

write-down

A reduction in the recorded value of an item of stock to comply with the principle of valuing stock at the lower of cost or net realisable value; may also be applied to investments and fixed assets.

Section 3

OPERATING TERMS

available hours
The number of hours for which a worker or machine is available for work. In a simple case for a worker this could be as follows for a 4 week period:

		Hours
Number of contractual hours		140
Overtime hours		20
Absence:		
Public holidays	7	
Annual holidays	28	
Certified sickness	2	
Other absence	13	
	—	(50)
Available hours		110

bought out stock
Any component bought outside the entity for incorporation in manufactured goods. *See also* factored goods.

breaking-down time
The time required to return a work station to a standard condition after completion of an operation (BS 5191).

by-product
A product which is recovered incidentally from the material used in the manufacture of recognised main products, such a by-product having either a net realisable value or a usable value which is relatively low in comparison with the saleable value of the main products.

By-products may be further processed to increase their realisable value. *See also* joint products.

changeover time
The time required to change a work station from a state of readiness for one operation to a state of readiness for another (BS 5191).

closed system
A system that operates without outside intervention. Applicable to routine systems. *See* feedback.

cycle time
The time required to complete an operation on one unit (BS 5191).

direct hours
The hours of employees applied directly to a product or service.

diverted hours
The available hours of nominally direct workers which are diverted to indirect activities, e.g. cleaning machines, and are therefore charged as indirect labour.

The alternative expressions *directs on indirect work*, *indirect hours* or *diversions* are not recommended. Note the distinction between a nominated direct worker and an indirect worker whose entire time is charged as indirect wages.

down time
The period of time for which a work station is not available for production due to a functional failure (BS 5191). *See also* idle time.

economic order quantity
A quantity of materials to be ordered which takes into account the optimum combination of :
1. bulk discounts from high volume purchases,
2. usage rate,
3. stock holding costs,
4. storage capacity,
5. order delivery time,
6. cost of processing the order.

factored goods
Goods bought in for resale.

finished goods
Manufactured goods, ready for sale or despatch, e.g. to a customer or agent.

idle time
The period of time for which a work station is available for production but is not utilised due to shortage of tooling, material, operators, etc. (BS 5191). *See also* waiting time.

joint products
Two or more products separated in the course of processing, each having a sufficiently high saleable value to merit recognition as a main product. *See also* by-product.

operation time
The period of time required to carry out an operation on a complete batch exclusive of set-up and breaking-down times (BS 5191).

perpetual inventory
The recording as they occur of receipts, issues, and the resulting balances of individual items of stock in either quantity or quantity and value.

physical inventory
An inventory determined by actual count, weight or measurement.

process time
The period of time which elapses between the start and finish of one process or stage of a process.

raw material
Unprocessed stock awaiting conversion.

rejects
Units of output which fail to reach the required standard of quality or specification before despatch to customers or subsequent users.
Such faulty units may be capable of rectification, and may be so corrected if the cost of doing so is less than the loss in value from allowing the fault to remain uncorrected. When it is uneconomic to rectify a fault, the article may be sold as sub-standard if it is still functionally sound; otherwise it may be disposed of as scrap.

returns
Goods returned by the customer to a supplier, e.g. because they do not meet the required quality, or specification or the quantity is incorrect, or they have been damaged in transit.

scrap
Discarded material which has some recovery value and which is usually either disposed of without further treatment (other than reclamation and handling), or reintroduced into the production process in place of raw material.

set-up time
The time required to prepare a work station from a standard condition to readiness to commence a specified operation (BS 5191).

stock
Any current asset held for conversion into cash in the normal course of trading, e.g. raw materials, work in progress, finished goods and goods in transit, or on consignment, or on sale or return.

stock account
An account in a ledger in value and sometimes also in quantity containing separately identifiable classes of materials, e.g. work in progress, indirect materials and finished goods.

terotechnology
A combination of management, financial, engineering and other practices, applied to physical assets in pursuit of economic life cycle costs, i.e. its aim is to obtain the best use of physical assets at the lowest total cost to the entity.

transit time
The period of time between the completion of an operation and the availability of the material at the succeeding work station (BS 5191).

waiting time
The period of time for which an operator is available for production but is prevented from working by shortage of material or tooling, machine breakdown (BS 5191). *See also* idle time.

waste
Discarded substances having no value (as distinct from scrap).

work in progress
Any material, component, product or contract at an intermediate stage of completion.

Section 4

COST CONCEPTS, METHODS
AND TECHNIQUES

absorbed overhead

Overhead which, by means of absorption rates, is included in costs of specific products or saleable services, in a given period of time.

Under or over-absorbed overhead. The difference between overhead cost incurred and overhead cost absorbed: it may be split into its two constituent parts for control purposes. *See* overhead expenditure variance and overhead volume variance.

absorption costing

A principle whereby fixed as well as variable costs are allotted to cost units and total overheads are absorbed according to activity level.

The term may be applied where (a) production costs only, or (b) costs of all functions are so allotted. *See* figure 4.6.

absorption rate

A rate applied to a unit of production which is intended to account for the overhead applicable to a standard production volume.

avoidable costs

Those costs which can be identified with an activity or sector of a business and which would be avoided if that activity or sector did not exist.

bases of apportionment

Formulae varying according to the nature of costs for the purpose of apportioning those costs among cost centres or products.

Typical bases of apportionment for budgeted overhead and an illustration of a combination of allocation and apportionment are set out in figure 4.10.

basic costing method

A method of costing which is devised to suit the methods by which goods are manufactured or services are provided.

batch cost

Aggregated costs relative to a cost unit which consists of a group of similar articles which maintains its identity throughout one or more stages of production.

batch costing
That form of specific order costing which applies where similar articles are manufactured in batches either for sale or for use within the undertaking.

In most cases the costing is similar to job costing. *See* figure 4.6.

capital investment appraisal
The process of evaluating proposed investment in specific fixed assets and the benefits to be obtained from their acquisition.

The techniques used in the evaluation can be summarised as non-discounting methods (i.e. simple pay-back), return on capital employed and discounted cash flow methods, (i.e. yield, net present value and discounted pay-back).

common costs
Shared costs of more than one product or service, where the shared proportions are determined by management decision.

concept: social responsibility cost
Tangible and intangible costs and losses sustained by third parties or the general public as a result of unrestrained economic activity, e.g. pollution of rivers by industrial effluent.

concept: sunk cost
Assets which can continue to serve their present purpose but which have no significant resaleable value for another purpose.

continuous operation/process costing
The basic costing method applicable where goods or services result from a sequence of continuous or repetitive operations or processes to which costs are charged before being averaged over the units produced during the period. *See* figure 4.6.

contract cost
Aggregated costs relative to a single contract designated a cost unit.

This usually applies to major long term contracts as distinct from short term job costs.

contract costing
That form of specific order costing which applies where work is undertaken to customers' special requirements and each order is of long duration (compared with those to which job costing applies).

The work is usually constructional and in general the method is similar to job costing. *See* figure 4.6.

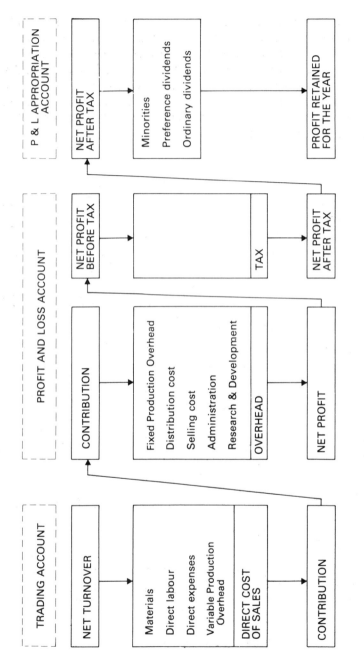

Figure 4.1 Contribution – derivation of profit using marginal costing
(See figure 10.5 for absorption costing)

contribution
The difference between sales value and the variable cost of those sales, expressed either in absolute terms or as a contribution per unit. This is a central term in marginal costing, when the contribution per unit is expressed as the difference between its selling price and its marginal cost. In turn this is then often related to a key or limiting factor to give a sum required to cover fixed overhead and profit, such as contribution per machine hour, per direct labour hour or per kilo of scarce raw material. *See* figure 4.1.

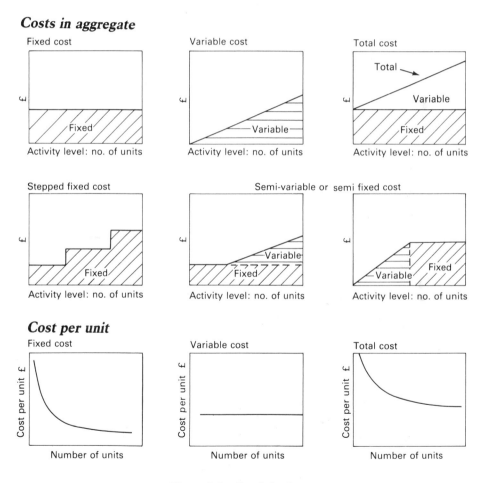

Figure 4.2 Cost behaviour

controllable or managed cost

A cost, chargeable to a budget or cost-centre, which can be influenced by the actions of the person in whom control of the centre is vested.

It is not always possible to pre-determine responsibility, because the reason for deviation from expected performance may only become evident later. For example, excessive scrap may arise from inadequate supervision or from latent defect in purchased material.

conversion cost

Costs of converting material input into semi-finished or finished products, i.e. additional direct materials, direct wages, direct expenses and absorbed production overhead.

cost allocation

The charging of discrete identifiable items of cost to cost centres or cost units. *See* figure 4.10. Part of cost attribution.

cost apportionment

The division of costs amongst two or more cost centres in proportion to the estimated benefit received, using a proxy, e.g. square feet. *See* figure 4.10. Part of cost attribution.

cost ascertainment

The collection of costs attributable to cost centres and cost units using the costing methods, principles and techniques prescribed for a particular business entity.

cost attribution

The process of attributing cost to cost centre or cost units resulting from cost allocation and cost apportionment.

cost behaviour

The way in which costs per unit of output are affected by fluctuations in the level of activity. *See* figure 4.2.

Since these costs cannot always be precisely assessed they may be determined by the use of a scattergraph as shown in figure 4.3, or more precisely by regression techniques.

cost benefit analysis

The measurement of resources used in an activity and their comparison with the value of the benefit to be derived from the activity.

cost experience curve

The relationship plotted between cost per unit expressed in constant money terms, and cumulative units produced per unit – usually plotted on a double logarithmic scale. Also called *learning curve*. *See* figure 4.4.

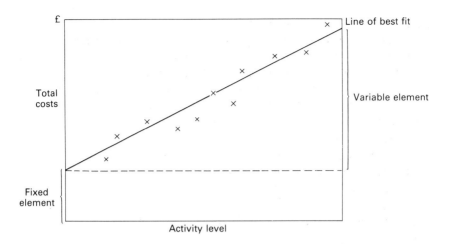

Figure 4.3 Assessment of fixed cost element by the use of scattergraph

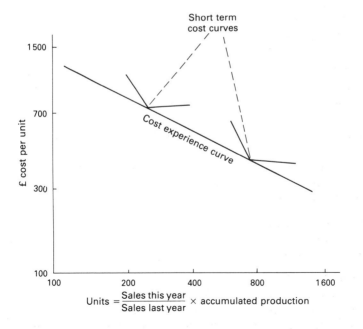

Figure 4.4 Cost experience curve

cost of capital
The cost of financing an investment, expressed as a percentage rate.
    The rate should be based on the overall pool of capital. *See also* weighted average cost of capital.

cost unit
A quantitative unit of product or service in relation to which costs are ascertained. *See* figure 4.5.

cost unit rate
A rate calculated by dividing the budgeted or estimated overhead cost attributable to a cost centre by either the number of cost units expected to be produced in that cost centre, or by the number related to working at normal capacity.

costing principles and techniques
Principles and techniques devised to suit the manner in which it is decided to present information to management. The relationship of costing principles, techniques and methods is shown in figure 4.6.

differential costing
A technique used in the preparation of ad hoc information in which only cost and income differences between alternative courses of action are taken into consideration.

direct labour cost percentage rate
A rate calculated by dividing the budgeted or estimated overhead cost attributable to a cost centre by the amount of direct labour cost expected to be incurred (or which would relate to working at normal capacity) and expressing the result as a percentage.

direct labour hour rate
A rate calculated by dividing the budgeted or estimated overhead cost attributable to a cost centre by the appropriate number of direct labour hours.
    Hours may be either the number of hours expected to be worked, or the number of hours which would relate to working at normal capacity.

discount rate (capital investment appraisal)
A percentage used to discount future cash flows generated by a capital project.
    Two rates commonly used are:
(a) internal rate of return,
(b) weighted average cost of capital.

Industry or activity	Cost unit
Manufacturing industries	
Abattoirs	1,000 head of cattle handled
Brewers	Barrel/hectolitre
Brick-making	1,000 bricks
Coal mining	Ton/tonne
Electricity	KWH
Gas	Therm
Iron/steel	Tonne/ton/cwt/sheet (a) Rolled (b) Cast (c) Extruded
Paper	Ream
Sand and gravel	Cubic yard/metre
Timber	100 ft./standard/stere
Weaving	100,000 picks
Service industries	
Hospitals	(a) Bed occupied (b) Out-patient
Local authority	£ of rateable value
Schools	1. Number of enrolled students 2. Number of successful students 3. Number of school meals
Swimming baths	Numbers of bathers
Professional service (accountants, auditors, lawyers, surveyors)	Chargeable man-hour
Individual organisations	
Personnel department and welfare	Employee
Materials storage/handling	(a) Requisition (b) Units issued/received (c) Values issued/received
Heating, lighting, rates, rent	Square feet/metres
Power	KWH
Salesmens' expenses	(a) £ of turnover (b) Calls made (c) Miles travelled (d) Orders taken (a) Number (b) Value
Sales ledger	Account maintained
Steam raising	1,000 pounds
Telephones	(a) Calls made (b) Number of extensions

Figure 4.5 Examples of commonly used cost units

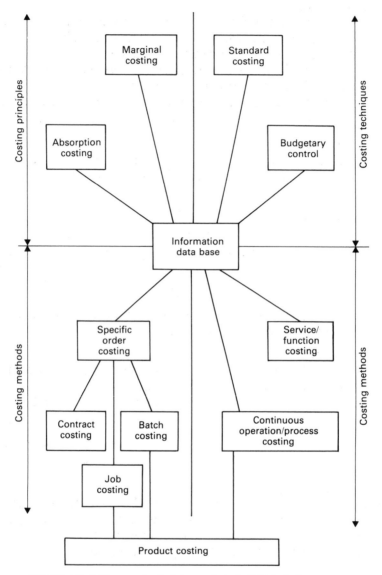

The above techniques and principles apply to both historical
cost and current cost accounting bases.

Figure 4.6   Costing principles, techniques and methods

discounted cash flow
An evaluation of the future net cash flows generated by a capital project, by discounting them to their present-day value.

The two methods most commonly used are:
(a) yield method, for which the calculation determines the internal rate of return (IRR) in the form of a percentage,
(b) net present value (NPV) method, in which the discount rate is chosen and the answer is a sum of money.

elements of cost
The constituent parts of costs according to the factors upon which expenditure is incurred viz, materials, labour and expenses. *See* figure 4.7.

equivalent units
A notional quantity of completed units substituted for an actual quantity of incomplete physical units in progress, when the aggregate work content of the incomplete units is deemed to be equivalent to that of the substituted quantity of completed units, e.g. 150 units 50 per cent complete = 75 equivalent units.

The principle applies when operation costs are being apportioned between work in progress and completed output.

expected value
The result of multiplying the financial forecast of the outcome of a course of action by the probability of achieving that outcome.

The probability is expressed as a figure between 0 and 1.

first in, first out price (FIFO)
A method of pricing material issues using the oldest purchase price first.

incremental costing
A technique used in the preparation of ad hoc information where consideration is given to a range of graduated or stepped changes in the level or nature of activity, and the additional costs and revenues likely to result from each degree of change are presented.

incremental yield
A measure used in capital investment appraisal where a choice lies between two or more projects.

The cash flows of project A are deducted from those of project B and the rate of return is calculated on the incremental cash flow.

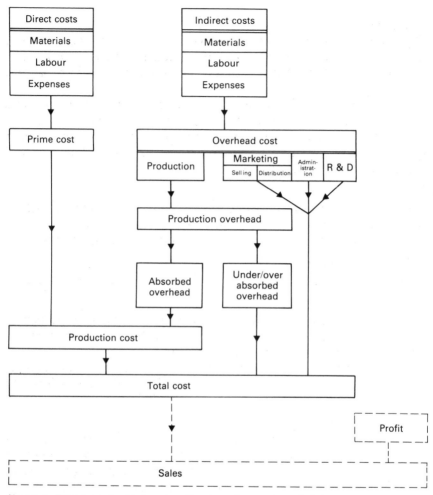

Notes: 1. The above chart is based on the absorption costing principle,
2. In the case of marginal costing, the amount of production overhead absorbed would relate to the variable element only.

Figure 4.7 Elements of cost

internal rate of return (IRR)

A percentage discount rate used in capital investment appraisal which brings the cost of a project and its future cash inflows into equality.

job cost

Aggregated costs relative to a cost unit which consists of a single specific customer order or specific task.

job costing
That form of specific order costing which applies where work is undertaken to customers' special requirements and each order is of comparatively short duration (compared with those to which contract costing applies).

The work is usually carried out within a factory or workshop and moves through processes and operations as a continuously identifiable unit. The term may also be applied to work such as property repairs and the method may be used in the costing of internal capital expenditure jobs. *See* figure 4.6.

joint costs
The costs of providing two or more products or services whose production could not, for physical reasons, be segregated.

Example, the cost of sheep rearing to produce both mutton and wool.

last in, first out price (**LIFO**)
A method of pricing material issues using the last purchase price first.

machine hour rate
A rate calculated by dividing the budgeted or estimated overhead or labour and overhead cost attributable to a machine or group of similar machines by the appropriate number of machine hours.

The hours may be the number of hours for which the machine or group is expected to be operated, the number of hours which would relate to normal working for the factory, or full capacity.

margin
An expression used to denote the difference in unit value percentage, or total value, between realised sales and the cost of goods sold. Since the margin may be calculated at different stages, the terms *gross* and *net* margin are used to differentiate between the levels.

marginal cost
The variable cost of one unit of a product or a service, i.e. a cost which would be avoided if the unit was not produced or provided.

Note: In this context a unit is usually either a single article or a standard measure such as the litre or kilogram, but may in certain circumstances be an operation, process or part of an organisation.

marginal costing
A principle whereby variable costs are charged to cost units and the fixed cost attributable to the relevant period is written off in full against the contribution for that period. *See* figure 4.6.

net present value (NPV)
The value obtained by discounting all cash outflows and inflows attributable to a capital investment project by a chosen percentage, e.g. the entity's weighted average cost of capital.

non-controllable cost (indirectly controlled cost)
A cost chargeable to a budget or cost centre which can only be influenced indirectly by the actions of the person in whom control of the centre is vested (*see* note following definition of controllable cost).

Typically, these costs will be mainly an apportionment of overhead costs of the entity.

notional cost
A hypothetical cost taken into account in a particular situation to represent a benefit enjoyed by an entity in respect of which no actual expense is incurred.

opportunity cost
The value of a benefit sacrificed in favour of an alternative course of action.

overhead absorption methods
The charging of overhead to cost units by means of rates separately calculated for each cost centre.

In most cases the rates are predetermined.

payback
The period, usually expressed in years, which it takes the cash inflows from a capital investment project to equal the cash outflows.

When deciding between two or more competing projects the usual decision is to accept the one with the shortest payback. Payback is commonly used as a first screening method. It is a rough measure of liquidity and not of profitability.

planned cost reduction
The reduction in unit cost of goods or services without impairing suitability for the use intended.

Cost reduction can be tackled by:
1. assigning cost reduction to an existing department,
2. creating a new department,
3. forming a committee,
4. using outside consultants,
5. initiating a short campaign by a large number of people,
6. appointing a team of experts from within the company, relieving them of their normal work for a short time.

All functions and activities of the entity may be examined, but especially design, production organisation and methods, marketing and finance, and investigations seek answers to the following questions:

(a) what is done, where, when, by whom, how and why,

(b) what are the possible cheaper alternatives, and what is the most suitable choice?

policy costs

Costs incurred as a result of taking a particular policy decision.

For example, ownership of assets will create a charge for depreciation. Depreciation is therefore a policy cost.

present value

The cash equivalent now of a sum of money receivable or payable at a stated future date at a specified rate. *See* figure 4.8.

product cost

The cost of a finished product built up from its cost elements.

An example of a product cost which provides for a first estimate, a subsequent standard cost and for stock valuations at various work in progress stages is given in figure 4.9.

relevant costs

Costs appropriate to aiding the making of specific management decisions.

replacement price

The price at which material identical to that which is to be replaced could be purchased at the date of valuation (as distinct from actual cost price at actual date of purchase).

semi-variable cost/semi-fixed cost

A cost containing both fixed and variable elements, and which is thus partly affected by fluctuations in the level of activity.

service/function costing

The costing of specific services or functions, e.g. canteens, maintenance, personnel. These may be referred to as service centres, departments or functions. *See* figure 4.6.

specific order costing

The basic costing method applicable where the work consists of separate contracts, jobs or batches, each of which is authorised by a special order or contract. *See* figure 4.6.

Years hence	1%	2%	4%	6%	8%	10%	12%	14%	15%	16%	18%	20%	22%	24%	25%	26%	28%	30%	35%	40%	45%	50%
1	0.990	0.980	0.962	0.943	0.926	0.909	0.893	0.877	0.870	0.862	0.847	0.833	0.820	0.806	0.800	0.794	0.781	0.769	0.741	0.714	0.690	0.667
2	0.980	0.961	0.925	0.890	0.857	0.826	0.797	0.769	0.756	0.743	0.718	0.694	0.672	0.650	0.640	0.630	0.610	0.592	0.549	0.510	0.476	0.444
3	0.971	0.942	0.889	0.840	0.794	0.751	0.712	0.675	0.658	0.641	0.609	0.579	0.551	0.524	0.512	0.500	0.477	0.455	0.406	0.364	0.328	0.296
4	0.961	0.924	0.855	0.792	0.735	0.683	0.636	0.592	0.572	0.552	0.516	0.482	0.451	0.423	0.410	0.397	0.373	0.350	0.301	0.260	0.226	0.198
5	0.951	0.906	0.822	0.747	0.681	0.621	0.567	0.519	0.497	0.476	0.437	0.402	0.370	0.341	0.328	0.315	0.291	0.269	0.223	0.186	0.156	0.132
6	0.942	0.888	0.790	0.705	0.630	0.564	0.507	0.456	0.432	0.410	0.370	0.335	0.303	0.275	0.262	0.250	0.227	0.207	0.165	0.133	0.108	0.088
7	0.933	0.871	0.760	0.665	0.583	0.513	0.452	0.400	0.376	0.354	0.314	0.279	0.249	0.222	0.210	0.198	0.178	0.159	0.122	0.095	0.074	0.059
8	0.923	0.853	0.731	0.627	0.540	0.467	0.404	0.351	0.327	0.305	0.266	0.233	0.204	0.179	0.168	0.157	0.139	0.123	0.091	0.068	0.051	0.039
9	0.914	0.837	0.703	0.592	0.500	0.424	0.361	0.308	0.284	0.263	0.225	0.194	0.167	0.144	0.134	0.125	0.108	0.094	0.067	0.048	0.035	0.026
10	0.905	0.820	0.676	0.558	0.463	0.386	0.322	0.270	0.247	0.227	0.191	0.162	0.137	0.116	0.107	0.099	0.085	0.073	0.050	0.035	0.024	0.017
11	0.896	0.804	0.650	0.527	0.429	0.350	0.287	0.237	0.215	0.195	0.162	0.135	0.112	0.094	0.086	0.079	0.066	0.056	0.037	0.025	0.017	0.012
12	0.887	0.788	0.625	0.497	0.397	0.319	0.257	0.208	0.187	0.168	0.137	0.112	0.092	0.076	0.069	0.062	0.052	0.043	0.027	0.018	0.012	0.008
13	0.879	0.773	0.601	0.469	0.368	0.290	0.229	0.182	0.163	0.145	0.116	0.093	0.075	0.061	0.055	0.050	0.040	0.033	0.020	0.013	0.008	0.005
14	0.870	0.758	0.577	0.442	0.340	0.263	0.205	0.160	0.141	0.125	0.099	0.078	0.062	0.049	0.044	0.039	0.032	0.025	0.015	0.009	0.006	0.003
15	0.861	0.743	0.555	0.417	0.315	0.239	0.183	0.140	0.123	0.108	0.084	0.065	0.051	0.040	0.035	0.031	0.025	0.020	0.011	0.006	0.004	0.002
16	0.853	0.728	0.534	0.394	0.292	0.218	0.163	0.123	0.107	0.093	0.071	0.054	0.042	0.032	0.028	0.025	0.019	0.015	0.008	0.005	0.003	0.002
17	0.844	0.714	0.513	0.371	0.270	0.198	0.146	0.108	0.093	0.080	0.060	0.045	0.034	0.026	0.023	0.020	0.015	0.012	0.006	0.003	0.002	0.001
18	0.836	0.700	0.494	0.350	0.250	0.180	0.130	0.095	0.081	0.069	0.051	0.038	0.028	0.021	0.018	0.016	0.012	0.009	0.005	0.002	0.001	0.001
19	0.828	0.686	0.475	0.331	0.232	0.164	0.116	0.083	0.070	0.060	0.043	0.031	0.023	0.017	0.014	0.012	0.009	0.007	0.003	0.002	0.001	
20	0.820	0.673	0.456	0.312	0.215	0.149	0.104	0.073	0.061	0.051	0.037	0.026	0.019	0.014	0.012	0.010	0.007	0.005	0.002	0.001	0.001	
21	0.811	0.660	0.439	0.294	0.199	0.135	0.093	0.064	0.053	0.044	0.031	0.022	0.015	0.011	0.009	0.008	0.006	0.004	0.002	0.001		
22	0.803	0.647	0.422	0.278	0.184	0.123	0.083	0.056	0.046	0.038	0.026	0.018	0.013	0.009	0.007	0.006	0.004	0.003	0.001	0.001		
23	0.795	0.634	0.406	0.262	0.170	0.112	0.074	0.049	0.040	0.033	0.022	0.015	0.010	0.007	0.006	0.005	0.003	0.002	0.001			
24	0.788	0.622	0.390	0.247	0.158	0.102	0.066	0.043	0.035	0.028	0.019	0.013	0.008	0.006	0.005	0.004	0.003	0.002	0.001			
25	0.780	0.610	0.375	0.233	0.146	0.092	0.059	0.038	0.030	0.024	0.016	0.010	0.007	0.005	0.004	0.003	0.002	0.001	0.001			
26	0.772	0.598	0.361	0.220	0.135	0.084	0.053	0.033	0.026	0.021	0.014	0.009	0.006	0.004	0.003	0.002	0.002	0.001				
27	0.764	0.586	0.347	0.207	0.125	0.076	0.047	0.029	0.023	0.018	0.011	0.007	0.005	0.003	0.002	0.002	0.001	0.001				
28	0.757	0.574	0.333	0.196	0.116	0.069	0.042	0.026	0.020	0.016	0.010	0.006	0.004	0.002	0.002	0.002	0.001	0.001				
29	0.749	0.563	0.321	0.185	0.107	0.063	0.037	0.022	0.017	0.014	0.008	0.005	0.003	0.002	0.002	0.001	0.001					
30	0.742	0.552	0.308	0.174	0.099	0.057	0.033	0.020	0.015	0.012	0.007	0.004	0.003	0.002	0.001	0.001	0.001					
40	0.672	0.453	0.208	0.097	0.046	0.022	0.011	0.005	0.004	0.003	0.001	0.001										
50	0.608	0.372	0.141	0.054	0.021	0.009	0.003	0.001	0.001	0.001												

Figure 4.8   Present value of one unit of currency

GARMENT COST AND STOCK VALUATION											
DESCRIPTION							STYLE				
							DATE				
FACTORY				SIZE			COMPILED				
CUSTOMER				REF			APPROVED				
		Quotation			Standard Cost			STOCK VALUATION			
CLOTH		QTY.	PRICE	COST	QTY.	PRICE	COST	1	2	3	4
1											
2											
3											
4											
5											
6											
CONTINGENCY AT	%										
A	TOTAL CLOTH COST										
TRIM AND PACKING											
1											
2											
3											
4											
CONTINGENCY AT	%										
B	TOTAL TRIM & PACKING COST										
LABOUR		Est. mins	PENCE/ MIN.	COST	Std. mins.	PENCE/ MIN.	COST				
CUT	1										
	2										
	3										
MACHINE	4										
	5										
	6										
	7										
	8										
	9										
FINISH	10										
	11										
	12										
CONTINGENCY AT	%										
C	TOTAL LABOUR COST										
D OVERHEAD (% of C)											
E OUTWORK COST											
F WORKS COST (A+B+C+D+E)											
G REJECTS & RETURNS (% of F)				STAGE VALUE ADDED							
H PRODUCTION COST F+G				STOCK VALUATION							

	TARGET			ACTUAL		N PROFIT VARIANCE (J–I)	
	I PROFIT (% of)			J PROFIT			
	DISTRIBUTION			K DISTRIBUTION		STANDARD SALES PRICE (M–N)	
	DISCOUNT			L DISCOUNT			
2nds PRICE		SALES PRICE		M SALES PRICE		PROFIT/M/c HOUR	
% NET PROFIT/SALES				% GROSS PROFIT/SALES		GROSS PROFIT/Mc HR	

Figure 4.9 Product cost

OVERHEAD ALLOCATION AND APPORTIONMENT SCHEDULE

YEAR 19....

Overheads	Total £	Base	Units	Rate per unit	Machine shop A Units	Machine shop A £	Machine shop B Units	Machine shop B £	Assembly Units	Assembly £	Stores Units	Stores £	Engineering services Units	Engineering services £	General services Units	General services £	Marketing Units	Marketing £	Administration Units	Administration £	Research and development Units	Research and development £
					Production Departments						**Service Departments**						**Other functions**					
Indirect wages	105,770	(Allocated)	—	—	—	23,250	—	19,300	—	28,650	—	5,100	—	2,750	—	3,490	—	11,520	—	8,110	—	3,600
Consumable supplies	32,420	(Allocated)	—	—	—	9,450	—	12,640	—	3,670	—	1,840	—	2,230	—	1,060	—	510	—	200	—	820
Depreciation: Building	8,400	Floor area (sq. ft)	12,000	70p	2,400	1,680	2,200	1,540	1,800	1,260	1,400	980	800	560	750	525	1,600	1,120	420	294	630	441
Plant & machinery	23,100	Asset value (£000's)	275	£84	79	6,636	95	7,980	21	1,764	13	1,092	35	2,940	17	1,428	—	—	—	—	15	1,260
Insurance: Buildings	1,800	Floor area (sq. ft)	12,000	15p	2,400	360	2,200	330	1,800	270	1,400	210	800	120	750	112	1,600	240	420	63	630	95
Plant & machinery	11,000	Asset value (£000's)	275	£40	79	3,160	95	3,800	21	840	13	520	35	1,400	17	680	—	—	—	—	15	600
Rates	4,200	Floor area (sq. ft)	12,000	35p	2,400	840	2,200	770	1,800	630	1,400	490	800	280	750	262	1,600	560	420	147	630	221
Electricity	9,460	KW hrs (000's)	86	£110	14	1,540	20	2,200	10	1,100	6	660	10	1,100	8	880	4	440	8	880	6	660
Heating oil	7,800	Floor area (sq. ft)	12,000	65p	2,400	1,560	2,200	1,430	1,800	1,170	1,400	910	800	520	750	488	1,600	1,040	420	273	630	409
Carriage inwards	1,400	Value of mtl issues	£70,000	2p	30,000	600	28,500	570	6,100	122	—	—	—	—	—	—	—	—	—	—	—	—
Carriage outwards	4,960	Sales	—	—	—	—	—	—	—	—	—	—	—	—	—	—	—	4,960	—	—	5,400	108
First aid	6,120	Employees on site	340	£18	90	1,620	85	1,530	75	1,350	6	108	22	396	13	234	4	72	35	630	10	180
Subscriptions	315	Allocated	—	—	—	—	—	—	—	—	—	—	—	—	—	—	—	—	—	315	—	—
	216,745					£50,696		£52,090		£40,826		£11,910		£12,296		£9,159		£20,462		£10,912		£8,394

Transfer of Service Dept. costs

Stores Dept Consumable supplies		3,680	4,923	1,429	(11,910)	869	413	199	78	319
Engineering Services Dept M/c hrs (00's)	325 £40.51	135 5,469	145 5,874	45 1,822	Nil	(13,165)	—	—	—
General services D. labour hrs (00's)	450 £10.65	162 3,446	153 3,254	135 2,872	—	Nil	(9,572)	—	—
		£63,291	£66,141	£46,949	—	—	Nil	£20,661	£10,990	£8,713

	Hours	Rate	Hours	Rate	Hours	Rate
Overhead absorption rate						
Machine hours	13,500	£4.69	14,500	£4.56	—	—
Direct labour hours	—	—	—	—	13,500	£3.48

Figure 4.10 Cost allocation and apportionment

Note: The above schedule is not comprehensive; there are other overhead expenses and methods of apportionment.

This schedule would be used in the budget preparation process and data used to ascertain overhead absorption rates for departmental use. Not all the bases available have been illustrated, only machine hour rate and direct labour rate. These have been selected on the grounds that they are the dominant elements in the departments illustrated.

transfer price

A price related to goods or other services transferred from one process or department to another or from one member of a group to another.

The extent to which costs and profit are covered by the price is a matter of policy. A transfer price may, for example, be based upon:

Marginal cost
Full cost
Market price
Negotiated price

For further information see ICMA Management Accounting Guideline No. 1.

uniform costing

The use by several undertakings of the same costing systems, i.e. the same basic costing methods, principles and techniques.

value analysis

A systematic inter-disciplinary examination of factors affecting the cost of a product or service, in order to devise means of achieving the specified purpose most economically at the required standard of quality and reliability (BS 3138).

variable cost

A cost which tends to follow (in the short term) the level of activity.

variable overhead cost

Overhead cost which tends to vary with changes in the level of activity.

weighted average cost of capital

A percentage discount rate used in capital investment appraisal to calculate the net present value of the costs and future revenues of the project.

It is the average cost of the combined sources of finance (equity, debentures, bank loans) weighted according to the proportion each element bears to the total pool of capital available. Weighting is usually based on the current market valuations and current yields or costs. Example:

Capital	Market value		Rate		Cost
Equity	£800,000	×	10%	=	£80,000
Debt	£400,000	×	15%	=	£60,000
Total	£1,200,000				£140,000

Weighted average 11.67%

weighted average price
A method of pricing material issues using a price which is calculated by dividing the total cost of material in stock by the total quantity in stock.

Section 5

PLANNING CONCEPTS AND TERMS

capital funding planning
The process of selecting suitable funds to finance long term assets and working capital.

capital resource planning
The process of evaluating and selecting long term assets to meet strategies.

competitive position
The position established relative to competition of an entity or product within a market, as indicated by relative cost, price, market share and accumulated experience. Also referred to as *strategic position*.

contingency plan
A plan to be implemented only upon the occurrence of future events other than those contained in the plan.

Contingency plans may be prepared for possible favourable or unfavourable events. For action to be taken where sales may exceed or fall substantially below planned levels, they may be as shown in figure 5.1.

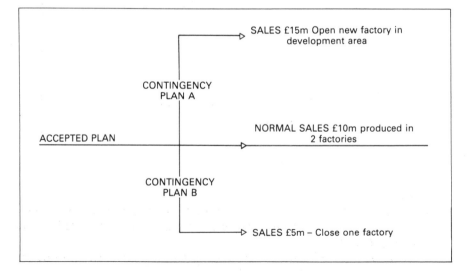

Figure 5.1 Contingency plan

As a second example, in relation to a possible unwanted takeover, planned action could be:
1. revalue buildings,
2. increase dividends,
3. release development plans.

corporate appraisal

A critical assessment of the strengths and weaknesses, opportunities and threats in relation to the internal and environmental factors affecting an entity in order to establish its condition prior to the preparation of the long term plan.

Sometimes referred to as *SWOT analysis*, after the relevant initial letters.

critical event

Any event which lies on the critical path.

critical path

The longest path or paths through a network. *See* figure 5.2.

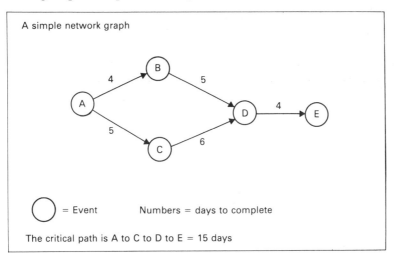

A simple network graph

◯ = Event   Numbers = days to complete

The critical path is A to C to D to E = 15 days

Figure 5.2   Critical path

decision tree

An analytical tool for clarifying for management the choices, risks, objectives, monetary gains and information needs involved in an investment problem.

It can be either non-quantitative for planning purposes, as in figure 5.3 or quantified for decision taking purposes.

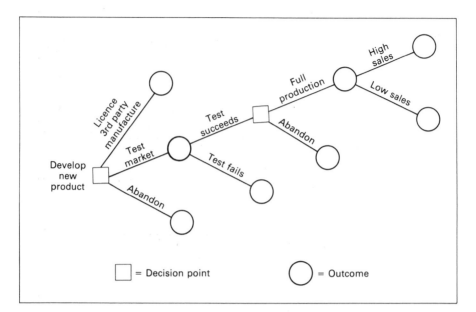

Figure 5.3   Decision tree

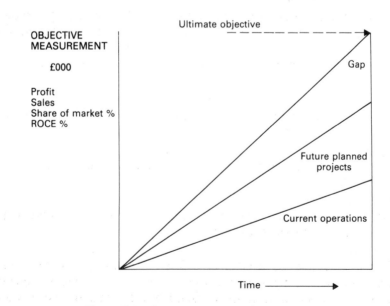

Figure 5.4   Gap analysis: identifying the gap

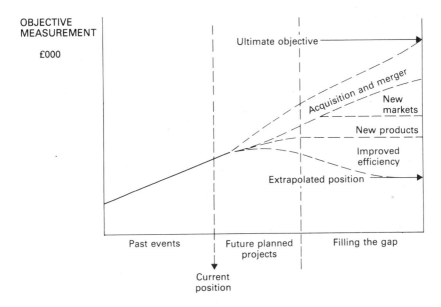

Figure 5.5 Gap analysis: filling the gap

dynamic programming

An operational research technique used to solve multi-stage problems in which the decisions at one stage are the accepted assumptions applicable to the next stage.

See also linear programming and non-linear programming.

event

The start or completion of an operation/activity.

In a network graph an event is represented by a small circle or node, and an activity by an arc.

extrapolation

The technique of determining a projection by statistical means. *See* figure 5.9.

financial planning

Planning in monetary terms of the acquisition and financing of resources and of their utilisation.

forecasting

The prediction of relevant future factors affecting an entity and its environment as a basis for formulation or reassessment of objectives and strategies and as a means to facilitate the preparation of planning decisions.

futuristic planning
   Planning for that period of time which extends beyond the planning horizon and which cannot usefully be expressed in quantified terms, but in the form of future expected conditions which will exist in respect of the entity, products/services and environment.
   For example, will motor cars be used in the long term future?

gap analysis
   A technique which attempts to analyse the 'gap' between the ultimate objective of the entity and its extrapolated existing performance by identifying the extent of the strategic task and the ways in which the gap might be closed.
   The entity's strengths and weaknesses, opportunities and threats are assessed and possible actions, such as expansion of production or other facilities, or the takeover of or merger with another corporate entity, are reviewed. *See* figures 5.4 and 5.5.

goal congruence
   The state that exists in a control system when it leads individuals and/or groups to take actions which are both in their self-interest and also in the best interest of the entity.

limiting factor or key factor
   A factor which at any time or over a period may limit the activity of an entity, often one where there is shortage or difficulty of supply.
   The limiting factor may change from time to time for the same entity or product. Thus, when raw materials are in short supply, performance or profit may be expressed as per kilo of material, or, in a restricted skilled labour market, as per skilled labour hour. Alternatively, the limiting factor may be one critical process in a chain.

linear programming
   The process of using a series of linear equations to construct a mathematical model, the objective of which is to obtain an optimal solution to a complex operational problem, given a number of alternative values of stated variables and quantitative constraints as to their use. *See also* dynamic programming and non-linear programming.

long term strategic planning
   The formulation, evaluation and selection of strategies involving a review of the objectives of an organisation, the environment in which it is to operate, and an assessment of its strengths, weaknesses, opportunities and threats for the purpose of preparing a long term strategic plan of action which will attain the objective set.

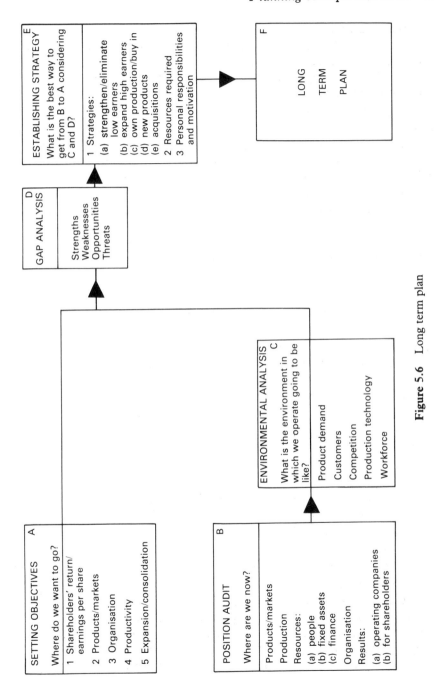

Figure 5.6 Long term plan

Where this applies to a corporate body, it may be referred to as corporate planning.

The expression long range planning is often used as an alternative to long term strategic planning. *See* figure 5.6.

market share

One entity's sales of a product or service in a specified market expressed as a percentage of total sales by all entities offering that product or service.

network analysis

A quantitative technique for the control of projects.

The events and activities making up the whole project are represented in the form of a graph. *See* critical path, and figure 5.2.

non-linear programming

A process in which the equations expressing the interactions of the variables are not all linear but may be, for example, in proportion to the square of a variable. *See* also linear programming and dynamic programming.

pareto (80/20) distribution

A frequency distribution with say 20 per cent of the items accounting for 80 per cent of the value/resources.

Common occurrences are:

1. sales, where 80 per cent of turnover arises from 20 per cent of customers,
2. stock, where 80 per cent of the value is represented by 20 per cent of the items. *See* figure 5.7.

PERT (project evaluation and review technique)

A specification of all activities, events and constraints relating to a project, from which a network is drawn which provides a model of the way the project should proceed.

planning

The establishment of objectives, and the formulation, evaluation and selection of the policies, strategies, tactics and action required to achieve these objectives.

Planning comprises long term/strategic planning, and short term operational planning. The latter usually refers to a period of one year.

planning horizon

The furthest time ahead for which plans can be usefully quantified with no more than a minimum acceptable degree of error.

It need not necessarily be the planning period.

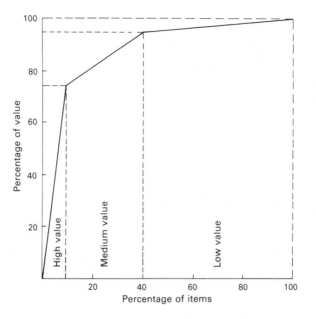

Figure 5.7 Pareto 80/20 distribution: stock

planning period

  The appropriate period of time which meets planning requirements and enables the decision making and/or control processes to be most effectively exercised.

  For example, forestry may require a period of many years whereas fashion garments may require only a few months.

position audit

  Part of the planning process which examines the present position of the entity in respect of:

  (a) its products and markets,
  (b) its production facilities,
  (c) its resources of people, fixed assets and finance,
  (d) its internal organisation,
  (e) results currently obtained from operating companies, and
  (f) the expectations of shareholders.

  See figure 5.6.

product life cycle

  The pattern of demand for a product or service over time. *See* figure 5.8.

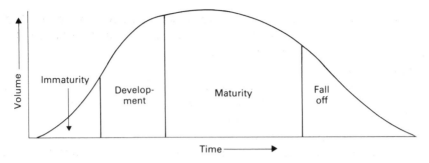

Figure 5.8 Product life cycle

projection

An expected future trend pattern obtained from existing data related to specific selected variables.

It differs from a forecast in that it is principally concerned with quantitative factors whereas a forecast includes judgements. *See* figure 5.9 and extrapolation.

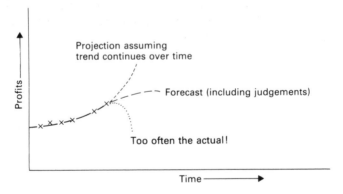

Figure 5.9 Projection

queueing time

The period of time between the arrival of material at a work station and the start of work on it (BS 5191).

rolling forecast

A continuously updated forecast covering one or more periods ahead, whereby each time actual results are reported a further forecast period is added and intermediate period forecasts are updated.

Often used to isolate underlying trends from seasonal or cyclical effects, so that both trends and effects are properly incorporated in the new forecast. *See also* rolling budget.

sensitivity analysis

A modelling procedure used in forecasting whereby changes are made in the estimates of the variables to establish whether any will critically affect the outcome of the forecast.

strategic management accounting

The provision and analysis of management accounting data relating to a business strategy: particularly the relative levels and trends in real costs and prices, volumes, market share, cash flow and the demands on a firm's total resources.

strategy

A course of action, including the specification of the resources required, to achieve a specific objective.

strategy: Boston classification

A classification developed by the Boston Consulting Group analysing products/businesses by market share and market growth.

In particular, *cash cow* refers to a product/business with a high market share and a low market growth, and *cash dog* refers to one with a low market share and low growth.

Section 6

CONTROL SYSTEMS AND BUDGETING

breakeven chart

A chart which indicates approximate profit or loss at different levels of sales volume within a limited range.

Figures 6.1 and 6.2 show examples of conventional breakeven charts. Figure 6.3 shows a contribution breakeven chart. In some entities there may be more than one breakeven point, and this is illustrated in figure 6.4.

breakeven point

The level of activity at which there is neither a profit nor loss.

This can be ascertained by various methods, including the use of a breakeven chart. The breakeven point may also be calculated by formulas, as follows:

$$\frac{\text{Total fixed cost}}{\text{Contribution per unit}} = \text{Number of units to be sold to breakeven (a)}$$

$$\frac{\text{Total fixed cost} \times \text{sales value}}{\text{Total contribution}} = \text{Sales value at breakeven point}$$

Alternatively, the sales value at breakeven point can be calculated: (a) × selling price per unit.

Example:

		£
Sales		10,000
Variable costs		
(direct materials, direct labour)		6,000
Contribution		4,000
Fixed cost		2,000
Profit		2,000

Number of units	1,000
Contribution per unit	£4

(a) $\dfrac{\text{Total fixed cost}}{\text{Contribution per unit}} = \dfrac{£2,000}{£4} = 500$ units to be sold to breakeven

(b) $\dfrac{\text{Total fixed cost} \times \text{sales value}}{\text{Total contribution}} = \dfrac{£2,000 \times £10,000}{£4,000} = £5,000 \text{ sales value at breakeven point}$

(c) Number of units at breakeven point × selling price per unit = 500 × £10 = £5,000 sales value at breakeven point.

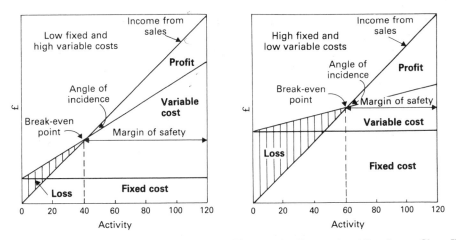

Figure 6.1 Conventional Breakeven Chart I **Figure 6.2** Conventional Breakeven Chart II

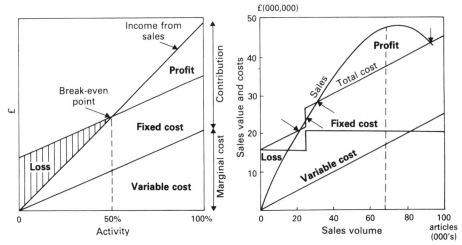

Break-even points are shown by arrows

Figure 6.3 Contribution Breakeven Chart **Figure 6.4** Multi-Breakeven Point Chart

budget

A plan quantified in monetary terms, prepared and approved prior to a defined period of time, usually showing planned income to be generated and/or expenditure to be incurred during that period and the capital to be employed to attain a given objective. *See* figures 6.7, 6.8 and 6.9 for examples of budget formats.

budget cost allowance

The cost which a budget centre is expected to incur in a control period.

At its simplest this usually comprises variable costs in direct proportion to the volume of production or service achieved, and fixed costs as a proportion of the annual budget.

budget period

The period for which a budget is prepared and used, which may then be sub-divided into control periods.

budgetary control

The establishment of budgets relating the responsibilities of executives to the requirements of a policy, and the continuous comparison of actual with budgeted results, either to secure by individual action the objective of that policy or to provide a basis for its revision. *See* figure 4.6.

capital expenditure authorisation

Formal authority to incur capital expenditure which meets the criteria defined to achieve the results laid down under a system of capital appraisal.

Levels of authority must be clearly defined and the reporting structure of actual expenditure must be to the equivalent authority levels. *See* the combined proposal and authorisation forms, figures 6.10 and 6.11.

capital expenditure budget

A plan for capital expenditure in monetary terms.

capital expenditure control

Procedures for the control of capital expenditure through prior authorisation on a formal proposal basis, and monitoring as expenditure is incurred. *See* figure 6.12.

capital expenditure proposal

A formal request for authority to incur capital expenditure.

This is usually supported by the case for the expenditure in accordance with capital investment appraisal criteria.

cash flow budget
A detailed budget of income and cash expenditure incorporating both revenue and capital items.
The cash flow budget should be prepared in the same format in which the actual position is to be presented. *See* figure 10.1. The year's budget is usually phased into shorter periods for control, e.g. monthly or quarterly.

control and monitoring
The continuous comparison of actual results with those planned, both in total and for separate sub-divisions and taking management action to correct adverse variances or to exploit favourable variances.

control limits
Limits in a system of exceptions reporting, in quantities or value, outside which special managerial action is triggered. For example:
1. Budgeted output 5,000 units per week: if actual output is between an upper limit of 5,200 and a lower limit of 4,800 units, no action is required.
2. Budget expenditure £10,000, upper limit £10,500, lower limit £9,500: an actual expenditure of £11,000 would require corrective action.

control period
A period in respect of which comparisons are made between budget and actual results.

cut-off
A date and procedure selected for isolating the flow of cash and goods, stock-taking and the related documentation, to ensure that all aspects of a transaction are dealt with in the same financial period.

departmental/functional budget
A budget of income and/or expenditure applicable to a particular function.
A function may refer to a department or a process. Functional budgets frequently include:
production cost budget (based on a forecast of production and plant utilisation),
marketing cost budget,
personnel budget,
purchasing budget,
research and development budget.

exceptions reporting

A system of reporting based on the exception principle which focuses attention on those items where performance differs significantly from standard or budget.

feedback

Modification or control of a process or system by its results or effects, by measuring differences between desired and actual results.

Feedback is an element in a feedback system and forms the link between planning and control. This can be illustrated by a simple central heating system, where differences between planned and actual temperatures are used as signals to effect automatic control, as shown in figure 6.5.

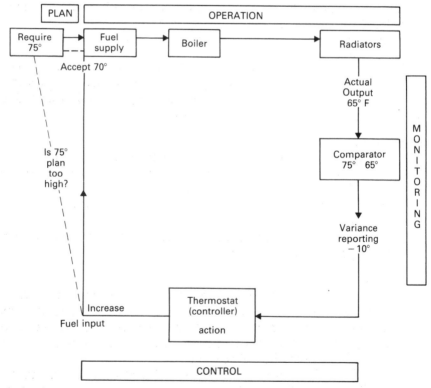

In the above, a system which operates without outside intervention (as the solid arrow lines) is termed a CLOSED SYSTEM and one that requires periodic outside adjustments to the planned or actual inputs an OPEN SYSTEM (dotted lines).

Figure 6.5   Feedback

feedback periods

The frequency of transmitting feedback information to the control function, which will be determined by such factors as the likelihood of the process going out of control, availability of information and cost of collection.

financial control

The use of management accounting information, the comparison of planned and actual performance and taking action to correct adverse trends or optimise favourable conditions.

This is not to be confused with the control of finance, which is the main function of treasurership.

fixed budget

A budget which is designed to remain unchanged irrespective of the volume of output or turnover attained.

flexible budget

A budget which, by recognising the difference in behaviour between fixed and variable costs in relation to fluctuations in output, turnover, or other variable factors such as number of employees, is designed to change appropriately with such fluctuations.

internal check

The procedures designed to provide assurance that:
(a) all the transactions and other accounting information which should be recorded have in fact been recorded,
(b) errors or irregularities in processing accounting information will become apparent,
(c) assets and liabilities recorded in the accounting system exist and are recorded at the correct amounts.

internal control system

The whole system of controls, financial and otherwise, established by the management in order to carry on the business of the enterprise in an orderly and efficient manner, ensure adherence to management policies, safeguard the assets and secure as far as possible the completeness and accuracy of the records.

The individual components of an internal control system are known as controls or internal controls.

long term budget

A long term plan usually prepared in monetary terms.

management audit

An objective and independent appraisal of the effectiveness of managers and the effectiveness of the corporate structure in the achievement of company objectives and policies.

Its aim is to identify existing and potential management weaknesses within an organisation and to recommend ways to rectify these weaknesses. *See also* audit: external and audit: internal.

margin of safety

The excess of normal or actual sales over sales at breakeven point.

See figures 6.1 and 6.2 and margin of safety ratio.

master budget

A budget which is prepared from, and summarises, the functional budgets. The term *summary budget* is synonymous.

noise

The overloading of the feedback process through the inclusion of irrelevant or insignificant data which can operate to confuse and divert attention from relevant information.

The more efficient the system the higher becomes the ratio of information to noise. In computer use noise is defined as unwanted signals present in electronic and electrical devices.

open system

A system that requires periodic outside adjustments to the planned inputs. Applicable to adaptive systems.

operational control

The process of controlling operations and services in accordance with strategic and tactical plans.

principal budget factor

A factor which, at a particular time or over a period, will limit the activities of an undertaking and which is therefore taken into account in preparing budgets. *See* limiting factor.

rolling budget

The continuous updating of a short term budget by adding, say, a further month or quarter and deducting the earliest month or quarter so that the budget can reflect current conditions.

Such procedures are beneficial where future costs and/or activities cannot be forecast with any degree of accuracy. *See also* rolling forecast.

routine control

Repetitive procedures of comparing feedback information with defined standards and acting to correct deviations.

short term budget
A budget established for use over a short period of time (usually one year but sometimes less) and which the person responsible is expected to achieve and use for control purposes.

short term tactical planning/budgeting
The process of preparing a short term and detailed plan of the activities of an organisation and so converting the strategic long term plan into action.

Those parts of a short term plan to which monetary values can be attached become budgets. For example, the production plan will deal with physical resources and output, and will become a production budget when it is expressed in monetary terms.

stock control
The systematic regulation of stock levels with respect to quantity, cost and lead time.

The alternative term *inventory control* is common in the USA. *See also* economic order quantity.

stock reorder level
A quantity of materials fixed in advance at which level stocks should be reordered.

stocktaking
A process whereby stocks (which may comprise direct and indirect materials, work in progress and finished goods) are physically counted and are then valued item by item.

This may be as at a point in time (periodic) or by counting and valuing a number of items at different times (continuous).

tactical planning
Planning the utilisation of resources in a manner most appropriate to the prevailing conditions, to achieve specific objectives in the most effective and efficient way.

tactics
The most efficient deployment of resources in an agreed strategy.

Early definitions of strategy and tactics limited them to military purposes, their first large scale organisational use. *See* figure 6.6.

zero base budgeting
A method of budgeting whereby all activities are re-evaluated each time a budget is formulated.

Each functional budget starts with the assumption that the function does not exist and is at zero cost. Increments of cost are compared with increments of benefit, culminating in the planned maximum benefit for a given budgeted cost.

EXAMPLE:	Army	Industry
Main objective	Defeat enemy	25% return on capital
Secondary objective	Preserve our forces	Increase market share
Strategy	Attack through border. Use 24,000 infantry.	Sell on the basis that a 20% increase in sales and production capacity will give a 25% reduction in costs. Use £10m capital.
Tactics	Send ¾ troops in first. Hold ¼ reserve. 12,000 infantry to seize ports at night. 6,000 to sever communications and 6,000 in reserve.	Drop selling prices now by 5%. Offer 5% bulk buying discounts.
Operational Control	Monitor progress towards ports. Redeploy if opposition stiffer than expected.	Monitor sales progress. Ensure machines and labour ready to take up 20% unused capacity.

Figure 6.6   Tactics

SALES BUDGET – YEAR ENDING . . .	Budget current year		Expected actual current year		Budget year	
	Qty	£000	Qty	£000	Qty	£000
1 *Sales – by customer* (Top 6 by name)						
1						
2						
3						
4						
5						
6						
Other outlets (grouped)						
1						
2						
3						
4						
5						
Sales of rejects/seconds						
Other sales						
A TOTAL SALES						
2 *Sales – by Product*						
Product						
1						
2						
3						
4						
5						
Other sales as above						
TOTAL AS A						
3 *Sales – by Reps/Agents*						
Name						
1						
2						
3						
4						
5						
6						
7						
TOTAL AS A						

Figure 6.7 Sales budget

PRODUCTION & DIRECT LABOUR BUDGET – YEAR ENDING . . . .

		Product →	Planned production – quantity				Totals	Key factors
			A	B	C	D		
1		Model P			22,500			
2		Model Q			42,500			
3								
4		Total / *Less:* Outside purchases			65,000 / 22,750			
5	1+2+3−4	Own manufacture			42,250			
6		Standard hrs needed — Per unit			10.0			
7	5 × 6	Standard hrs needed — Total hours			422,500		422,500	
8		Department	V	W	X	Y		
9		Standard hours needed in Dept.		211,250	211,250			
10	9 × 100 / 10	% Efficiency	%	%	70%	%	%	
11		Total attendance hours needed			301,786			
12		Total planned overtime hours			19,466			
13	11−12	Total normal hours required			282,320			
14		Normal Av. weekly hours per employee			39			Full time &/or part time
15		No. of working weeks in budgeted year			47.8			

			£	%	£	%	£	%
16	$\dfrac{13}{14 \times 15}$	No. of employees needed					151	%
17		Absentee rate %					5%	
18	$\dfrac{16 \times 100\%}{100\% - 17}$	No. of employees on payroll					159	

Gross wages cost

			£	£	£	£	£	£
19		Average weekly wage per employee					89.50	
20	16×19	Total normal wage bill per week					13,515	
21	$12 \times$ Rate	Overtime premium per week					1,200	
22		Other payments per week					—	
23	$20 + 21 + 22$	Total gross wages per week					14,715	
24	23×15	Total gross wages-budget year					703,377	

Employment costs

25	$20 \times$ Weeks	Holiday pay 4.2 weeks					56,763	
26		National Insurance					134,500	
27		Pensions					33,600	
28		Other					—	
29		Total employment cost					224,863	
30	$24 + 29$	Total gross wages + employment cost					928,240	

Figure 6.8 Production and direct labour budget

Note A: The budget for Department W would be calculated in the same way as Department X.

B: In practice total figures would be rounded to, say, the nearest £000, but in the example above have been left as calculated for ease of understanding.

C: The above calculations relate to manual workers, who are not paid when absent for reasons other than contractual holidays.

OVERHEAD EXPENSE BUDGET – YEAR ENDED . . . .

£000	Budget current year	Expected actual current year	Budget year	Cost centre apportionment				Basis of apportion-ment	Reasons for changes
				1	2	3	4		
Production overhead									
Indirect wages and salaries									
Related employment costs									
Power, light, heat and water									
Repairs:									
buildings									
machinery and plant									
Consumable stores									
Carriage inwards and works transport									
Works stationery									
Canteen costs									
Insurance									
Rent and rates									
Depreciation:									
buildings									
plant and machinery									
Sundry expenses									
Other									

Administration
Wages and salaries
Related employment costs
Telephone, telex and post
Bank charges
Audit fees
Other

Selling & Distribution
Wages and salaries
Related employment costs
Agents' commissions
Telephone, telex and post
Carriage outwards
Travelling expenses
Exhibition costs
Other

Figure 6.9 Overhead expense budget

CAPITAL EXPENDITURE PROPOSAL/AUTHORISATION

	Company/Unit

BRIEF DESCRIPTION OF PROPOSAL

	Proposal No.
	Date:
	Estimated Life years

TYPE

	tick box
Replacement	☐
Expansion	☐
Cost reduction	☐
Disposal	☐
Statutory	☐
Welfare	☐
Other	☐

A   EXPENDITURE TO BE INCURRED

Code	Description	Internal £000	External £000	Total £000
	Land			
	Buildings			
	Plant			
	Other			
	Less Grants			
	Less Realisation/Other Reductions			
	TOTAL	( )	( )	( )

B   WORKING CAPITAL INCREASE (DECREASE)

Stocks:
Direct materials
Work in progress
Finished goods
Debtors

Creditors

Net change

C TOTAL INVESTMENT = A + B

Method of financing
Purchase ☐ Hire ☐ Lease ☐ Attach quotation or proposal and full supporting details

Level of investment risk
High ☐ Medium ☐ Low ☐

AUTHORISATION CRITERIA
(Supported by detailed economic and environmental assumptions, marketing and cost statistics,
cash flow and risk analysis as per Case Statement attached)
* Discounted cash flow yield   %
* Net present value (state discounting %)   surplus/deficit/£000s
* Discounted pay back (state discounting %)   No. of years
* Average return on capital employed – first full year
  (Base Investment = B + 50% A)

%

Starting date   Completion date

Endorsement by company/unit
Name of proposer (block
letters) title and authority

Signed............   Date............

Authorisations	Authority level	Signature	Date
Approved/Rejected			
Approved/Rejected			

Figure 6.10 Capital expenditure proposal/authorisation

* These could be RANGES instead of SINGLE POINT FIGURES.

CAPITAL EXPENDITURE PROPOSAL/AUTHORISATION-VEHICLES

	Company/Unit
	Proposal No:
	Date:

BRIEF DESCRIPTION OF PROPOSAL

TYPE

tick box

- [ ] Replacement
- [ ] Expansion
- [ ] Cost reduction
- [ ] Statutory
- [ ] Other

DESCRIPTION AND MAKE OF VEHICLE(S)

ENGINE C.C.

INSURANCE
GROUP

METHOD OF FINANCING

A PURCHASE – Copy quote *must* be attached for vehicles not bring purchased under group arrangements

Full retail cost of vehicle and all extras
(excluding road tax)

Purchase discount

Net cost as attached quote   £

B HIRE OR LEASE

Annual hiring charge or lease rental
as attached proposal   £

Period of hire or lease

INCREMENTAL DCF YIELD AND NPV IN FAVOUR
OF [A] [B]   YIELD   %   NPV £
ATTACH DETAILED CASE SHOWING REASONS FOR PREFERRING A OR B

REPLACEMENT OR COST REDUCTION PROPOSALS

Details of vehicle(s) being replaced

Description and Make

Original Cost   £

Date of Purchase

Mileage – now
          expected at delivery date

Expected Sale/Trade-in value £

OTHER INFORMATION

APPROVAL	SIGNATURE	DATE
Approved at Subsidiary Co. by:		
Approved by Group Board Director:		

Figure 6.11   Capital expenditure proposal/authorisation-vehicles

CAPITAL EXPENDITURE CONTROL FORM

Quarter . . . .
Year . . . .

COMPANY/UNIT

Capital expend. approv. number	Description	Authorised	Actual expenditure and receipts			Bal. after 30 Sept.	Over (Under) spend		Comments
		Net cost	Total to 31 March	2nd Quarter	3rd Quarter	Net	Projected, against budget total	Actual to date against phased budget account	
			Net cost	Net cost	Net cost				
	TOTAL								
	Less Disposals								
	Balance sheet movements								

Enter cancellation proposals on separate form showing net costs and detailed effects

Figure 6.12   Capital expenditure control form

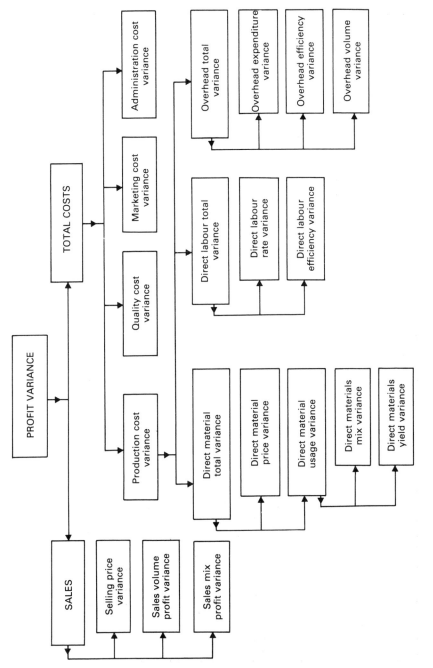

Figure 7.1 Variance analysis (absorption costing principles)

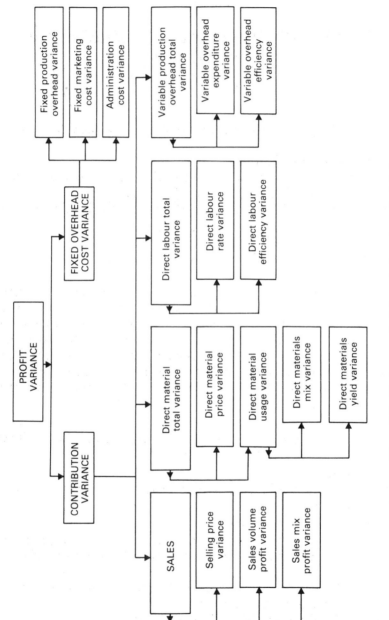

Figure 7.2 Variance analysis (marginal costing principles)

Section 7

STANDARD COSTING AND VARIANCE ACCOUNTING

Note: in the examples A = adverse variance, F = favourable variance.

administration cost variance
The difference between the budgeted cost of administration for a specified period and the actual expenditure incurred.
Formula: Budgeted administration costs – Actual administration costs
Example: £26,000 – £27,100 = £1,100 A
See appendix 7a.

attainable standard
A standard which can be attained if a standard unit of work is carried out efficiently, a machine properly operated or material properly used.
Allowances are made for normal shrinkage, waste and machine breakdowns. The standard represents future performance and objectives which are reasonably attainable. Besides having a desirable motivational impact on employees, attainable standards serve other purposes, e.g. cash budgeting, inventory valuation and budgeting departmental performance.

basic standard
A standard established for use over a long period from which a current standard can be developed.

current standard
A standard established for use over a short period of time, related to current conditions.

direct labour efficiency variance
The difference between the standard hours for the actual production achieved and the hours actually worked, valued at the standard labour rate.
Formula: (Standard hours produced – actual hours worked) × Standard rate per hour
Example: (11,000 – 12,500) × £2.0 = £3,000 A
See appendix 7a.

direct labour rate variance

The difference between the standard and the actual direct labour rate per hour for the total hours worked.

Formula: (Standard rate per hour − actual rate per hour) × Actual hours

Example: (£2.0 − £1.8) × 12,500 = £2,500 F

direct labour total variance

The difference between the standard direct labour cost and the actual direct labour cost incurred for the production achieved.

Formula: (Standard direct labour hours produced × standard rate per hour) − (Actual direct labour hours × actual rate per hour)

Example: (11,000 × £2) − (12,500 × £1.8) = £500 A

See appendix 7a.

direct material mix variance

Explanatory note: If a process uses several different materials which could be combined in a standard proportion, a mix variance can be calculated which shows the effect on cost of variances from the standard proportion.

There are two recognised ways of calculating this mix variance. Some authorities regard the variance as a sub-set of the usage variance but others treat it as part of the price variance.

If the mix variance is treated as a sub-set of the usage variance, then the definition and formula are:

Definition: The difference between the total quantity in standard proportion, priced at the standard price and the actual quantity of material used priced at the standard price.

Formula: (Quantity in standard mix proportions − Quantity in actual mix) × Standard price

See appendix 7b for example.

direct material price variance

The difference between the standard price and actual purchase price for the actual quantity of material. It can be calculated either at the time of purchase or at the time of usage. Generally, the former is preferable.

Formula: Actual quantity × (Standard price − Actual price)

Example: 12,000 × (£3 − £2.8333) = £2,000 F

See appendix 7a.

direct material total variance

The difference between the standard direct material cost of the actual production volume and the actual cost of direct material.

Formula: (Standard units × standard price) − (Actual units × actual
price)
Example: (11,000 × £3) − (12,000 × £2.8333) = £1,000 A
See appendix 7a.

direct material usage variance

The difference between the standard quantity specified for the actual
production and the actual quantity used, at standard purchase price.
Formula: (Standard quantity specified for actual production − actual
quantity used) × Standard price
Example: (11,000 − 12,000) × £3 = £3,000 A
See appendix 7a.

direct material yield variance

Explanatory note: Apart from operator or machine performance, output
quantities produced are often different to those planned, e.g. this
arises in chemical plants where plant should produce a given output
over a period for a given input but the actual output differs for a variety
of reasons.
Definition: The difference between the standard yield of the actual
material input and the actual yield, both valued at the
standard material cost of the product.
Formula: (Standard yield of actual input − Actual yield of
input) × Standard material cost.
See appendix 7b for example.

ideal standard

A standard which can be attained under the most favourable
conditions.

No provision is made, e.g. for shrinkage, spoilage or machine
breakdowns. Users believe that the resulting unfavourable variances
will remind management of the need for improvement in all phases of
operations. Ideal standards are not widely used in practice because they
may influence employee motivation adversely.

marketing cost variance

The difference between the budgeted costs of marketing (including
selling and distribution costs) and the actual marketing costs incurred
in a specified period.
Formula: Budgeted marketing costs − Actual marketing costs
Example: £25,000 − £25,900 = £900 A
See appendix 7a.

overhead efficiency variance

The difference between the standard overhead cost of the production achieved and the standard overhead cost of the actual hours taken.

Formula: (Standard hours for production achieved − Actual hours taken) × Standard overhead rate

Example: (11,000 − 12,500) × £1.5 = £2,250 A

See appendix 7a.

overhead expenditure variance

The difference between budgeted and actual overhead expenditure.

Budgeted overhead may be determined in different ways − it may be classed as totally fixed, or partly fixed and partly variable.

In the formula which follows, budgeted overhead has been determined as fixed overhead plus variable overhead for actual hours worked.

Formula: [Fixed overhead + (Actual hours × Standard variable overhead rate)] − Actual production overhead incurred

Example: £10,000 + (12,500 × £0.5) − £16,700 = £450 A

See appendix 7a.

overhead total variance

The difference between the standard overhead cost specified for the production achieved, and the actual overhead cost incurred.

Formula: (Standard variable overhead + Standard fixed overhead) − (Actual variable overhead + Actual fixed overhead)

Example: (£6,500 + £10,000) − (£6,100 + £10,600) = £200 A

Where overhead costs tend to vary with the amount of an input, e.g. actual labour hours, the overhead total variance may be subdivided into expenditure, efficiency and volume variances.

See appendix 7a.

overhead volume variance

The difference between the standard overhead cost of the actual hours taken and the flexed budget allowance for the actual hours taken.

Formula: (Actual hours × Standard overhead rate) − (Fixed overhead cost + [Actual hours × variable overhead rate])

Example: (12,500 × £1.5) − (£10,000 + [12,500 × £0.5]) = £2,500 F

See appendix 7a.

production cost variance

The difference between the standard production cost of actual production volume and the actual production cost over the specified period.

Formula: (Actual number of units produced × Standard production cost per unit = Standard production cost) − (Actual total cost of materials, wages and production overhead)

Example: (£71,500) − (£73,200) = £1,700 A

profit variance

The difference between the standard profit on the actual sales volume and the actual profit for a specific period.

Formula: (Standard profit) − (Actual profit)

Example: £31,500 − £38,800 = £7,300 F

See appendix 7a.

quality cost variance

The difference (arising from failure to conform to quality specification) between the amount included in standard costs and the actual cost or loss incurred in scrapping, rectifying, or selling at sub-standard prices.

Formula: (Number of units produced × Standard allowance per unit) − (Number of units rejected or returned × Cost per unit + Rectification cost − Disposal value)

If considered significant the variance can be further analysed into variances such as returns, customer allowances and production rejects.

revision variance

The difference between an original and a revised standard cost.

It arises when an interim adjustment of a standard cost is made without adjusting the budget, and is required to allow full analysis of the difference between budgeted and actual profit. The variance can be further analysed to reflect revisions to prices of materials, labour and overhead rates, and changes of method.

sales mix profit variance

The difference between total profit, calculated at individual product standard profit and at average standard profit, based on total actual units sold.

Formula: (Actual units sold at standard profit) − (Total units sold at average standard profit)

Example: For three products A, B and C, based on budgeted sales units, standard profits and actual sales units are as follows:

Product	Units	Profit per unit £	Total profit £	Average profit per unit £	Sales units
A	3,000	2.0	6,000		3,000
B	4,000	2.5	10,000		3,000
C	3,000	3.0	9,000		6,000
	10,000		25,000	2.5	12,000

(columns: Standard [Units, Profit per unit, Total profit, Average profit per unit] — Actual [Sales units])

(3,000 × £2) + (£3,000 × £2.5) + (6,000 × £3) − (12,000 × £2.5) = £1,500 F

(Actual units at standard profit) − (Total units at average standard profit).

Where sales are analysed by individual products or lines, a profit due to sales mix may be calculated: this may be more important than the selling price variance or the sales volume profit variance.

sales volume profit variance

The difference between the actual units sold and the standard quantity, priced at the standard profit per unit.

Formula: (Actual units − Standard units) × Standard profit

selling price variance

The difference between the actual selling price per unit and the standard selling price per unit multiplied by the actual quantity sold.

Formula: Actual units × (Actual selling price per unit − Standard selling price per unit)

Example: 11,000 units × (£15 − £14) = £11,000 F

See appendix 7a.

standard

A predetermined measurable quantity set in defined conditions against which actual performance can be compared, usually for an element of work, operation or activity.

While standards may be based on unquestioned and immutable natural law or facts, they are finally set by human judgement and consequently are subject to the same fallibility which attends all human activity. Thus a standard for 100 per cent machine output can be fixed by its geared input/output speeds, but the effective realisable output standard is one of judgement.

standard cost

A predetermined calculation of how much costs should be under specified working conditions.

It is built up from an assessment of the value of cost elements and correlates technical specifications and the quantification of materials, labour and other costs to the prices and/or wage rates expected to apply during the period in which the standard cost is intended to be used. Its main purposes are to provide bases for control through variance accounting, for the valuation of stock and work in progress and, in some cases, for fixing selling prices.

standard costing

A technique which uses standards for costs and revenues for the purpose of control through variance analysis. *See* figure 4.6.

standard direct labour cost

The planned average cost of direct labour for a specified amount of direct labour effort to be used at standard performance over a specified period. *See* standard performance.

Usually expressed as a cost per unit of time, i.e. standard hour or standard minute.

standard direct material cost

The predetermined cost price for a specified quantity of material to be used at a standard material usage rate over a specified period.

standard hour/minute

The quantity of work achievable at standard performance, expressed in terms of a standard unit of work in a standard period of time.

standard material usage

The quantity of material or rate of use required as an average, under specified conditions, to produce a specified quantity of output.

standard operating profit – unit

The predetermined profit from the sale of a specified unit of a product or service at the standard selling price.

standard overhead cost

The predetermined cost of overhead of a cost/revenue/profit centre over a specified period, using an agreed overhead absorption method: in marginal costing, this will be in respect of variable overhead only.

standard performance – labour

The rate of output which qualified workers can achieve as an average over the working day or shift, without over-exertion, provided they adhere to the specified method and are motivated to apply themselves to their work.

This is represented by 100 per cent on the BS scale (BS 3138).

standard performance – machine

The rate of output achievable by a machine as an average, under specified conditions over a given period of time.

It may include the standard performance of the operator.

standard price

A predetermined price fixed on the basis of a specification of a product or service and of all factors affecting that price.

standard production cost – total

The predetermined cost of producing or providing specified quantities of products or service at standard performance over a specified period.

standard production cost – unit

The predetermined cost of producing or providing a specified quantity of a product or service at standard performance.

standard profit – total

The predetermined profit arising from the sale of actual quantities of products or services at standard selling prices, over a specified period.

Formula: Actual number of units sold × (Standard selling price per unit − Standard cost per unit) = Standard profit

Example: 11,000 × (£14 − £11.1364)* = £31,500

Standard profit may be at the level of net profit, gross profit, or contribution. Profit which relates only to trading activities is often referred to as operating profit.

See appendix 7a.

* In practice this would probably be rounded to £11.14.

standard selling price – unit

A predetermined price for a product or service for a specified unit to be sold.

A unit may consist of a single item or a batch of processed output.

standard time
The total time (hours and minutes) in which a task should be completed at standard performance, i.e. basic time plus contingency allowance plus relaxation allowance.

standard unit of work
A unit of work consisting of basic time plus relaxation allowance and contingency allowance where applicable.
The unit of work may be for labour output only, a combination of machine and labour output, or for a machine only.

variance
The difference between planned, budgeted, or standard cost and actual costs (and similarly in respect of revenues).
Note: This is not to be confused with the statistical variance which measures the dispersion of a statistical population.

variance accounting
A technique whereby the planned activities of an undertaking are quantified in budgets, standard costs, standard selling prices and standard profit margins, and the differences between these and the actual results are compared.
The procedure is to collect, compare, comment and correct.

variance analysis
The analysis of variances arising in a standard costing system into their constituent parts.
It is the analysis and comparison of the factors which have caused the differences between pre-determined standards and actual results, with a view to eliminating inefficiencies. Appendix 7a shows a profit and loss statement in variance form and figure 7.1 shows the analysis of variances in diagrammatic form. The analysis is based on the assumption that a full (or absorption) costing system is being operated. Where a marginal (or variable) costing system is employed the variance analysis will take the form shown in figure 7.2. The significance of the contribution variance, which is the difference between the budgeted contribution and the actual contribution, should be noted.
In most organisations, other variances can be developed specifically related to the operations carried out in addition to those shown in figures 7.1, 7.2 and appendices 7a and 7b.

Appendix 7a

PROFIT AND LOSS ACCOUNT IN VARIANCE FORM

	£	£	£
SALES			165,000
			———
STANDARD PROFIT			31,500
VARIANCE			
Selling price variance		11,000 F	
Direct material:			
price variance	2,000 F		
usage variance	3,000 A		
total variance	———	1,000 A	
Direct labour:			
efficiency variance	3,000 A		
rate variance	2,500 F		
total variance	———	500 A	
Overhead:			
efficiency variance	2,250 A		
expenditure variance	450 A		
volume variance	2,500 F		
total variance	———	200 A	
Marketing cost variance		900 A	
Administration cost variance		1,100 A	
Profit variance		———	7,300 F
			———
ACTUAL PROFIT			38,800

Note:
1. In the above example, production quantities and sales quantities are the same.
2. F = favourable, A = adverse.

Appendix 7a

SUPPORTING INFORMATION FOR THE PROFIT AND LOSS ACCOUNT IN
VARIANCE FORM

	Budget	Flexed allowance	Standard	Actual	Variance
Sales:					
value	£140,000	+14,000 F	154,000	165,000	11,000 F
quantity	10,000		11,000	11,000	
unit price	£14		£14	£15	
Direct materials:					
value	£30,000	+3,000 A	33,000	34,000	1,000 A
quantity (sets)	10,000		11,000	12,000	
price	£3		£3	£2.8333	
Direct labour:					
value	£20,000	+2,000 A	22,000	22,500	500 A
hours	10,000		11,000	12,500	
rate	£2		£2	£1.8	
Production overhead:					
variable	£5,000	+1,500 A	6,500	6,100	200 A
fixed	£10,000		10,000	10,600	
	£15,000		16,500	16,700	
Rate per hour					
variable	£0.5		£0.5		
fixed	£1.0		£1.0		
Production cost of sales:					
value	£65,000		71,500	73,200	
per unit			£11.1364		
Marketing cost	£25,000		25,000	25,900	900 A
Administration cost	£26,000		26,000	27,100	1,100 A
Operating profit	£24,000	+£7,500 F	£31,500	£38,800	£7,300 F

Note: The column headed 'Flexed allowance' provides the link between the original budget for the manufacture and sale of 10,000 units and the standard applicable to the manufacture and sale of 11,000 units.

Appendix 7b

WORKED EXAMPLE OF MIX AND YIELD VARIANCES

1. *Initial data*

	Standard			Actual		
	Quantity in mix	Price	Value	Quantity in mix	Price	Value
	Kg	£/Kg	£	Kg	£/Kg	£
Material A	30,000	3.20	96,000	24,000	3.40	81,600
Material B	20,000	2.40	48,000	21,000	2.00	42,000
	50,000		144,000	45,000		123,600
4.5% Standard loss	2,250					
Output, product X	47,750			42,000		

2. *Procedure for calculating variances*
   (i) Express output in terms of standard cost content and value.
   (ii) Assess material cost variance in total.
   (iii) Sub-divide (ii) into price and usage variances.
   (iv) Further sub-divide usage variance into mix and yield variances.

3. *The results of the calculations and their relationship*

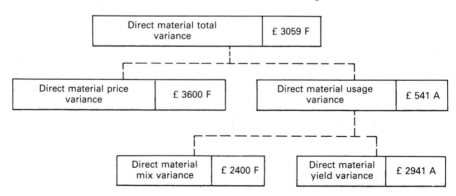

4. *The detailed calculations*

(a) Standard cost of standard mix

	£
Material A, 30,000 kgs at £3.20 per kg	96,000
Material B, 20,000 kgs at £2.40 per kg	48,000
	144,000

Yield = 47,750 kgs product X
∴ Standard cost of product X = £3.0157 per kg

(b) Standard cost of actual output of product X
    42,000 kgs × £3.0157 per kg = £126,659

(c) Actual cost of actual output

Material A, 24,000 kgs at £3.40 per kg	81,600
Material B, 21,000 kgs at £2.00 per kg	42,000
	123,600

(d) Direct material total variance

(b) − (c)
£126,659 − £123,600 =   £3,059 F

(e) Direct material price variance

Actual quantity × (Standard price − Actual price)
Material A, 24,000 kgs × (£3.20 − £3.40) =   £4,800 A
Material B, 21,000 kgs × (£2.40 − £2.00) =   £8,400 F

    Direct material price variance   £3,600 F

(f) Direct material usage variance

If there is a standard loss of 4.5%, an actual output of 42,000 kgs
would require a standard input of 43,979 kgs. This standard input of
43,979 should be in the following proportions:

60% Material A	26,387 kgs
40% Material B	17,592 kgs
	43,979 kgs

(Standard quantity − Actual quantity) × Standard price

Material A (26,387 kgs − 24,000 kgs) × £3.20 =	£7,638	F
Material B (17,592 kgs − 21,000 kgs) × £2.40 =	£8,179	A
Direct material usage variance	£541	A

(g) Direct material mix variance

Actual quantity used expressed in standard proportions.

Material A 60%	27,000 kgs
Material B 40%	18,000 kgs
	45,000 kgs

(Quantity in standard mix proportions − Quantity in actual mix) × Standard price

Material A (27,000 kgs − 24,000 kgs) × £3.20 =	£9,600	F
Material B (18,000 kgs − 21,000 kgs) × £2.40 =	£7,200	A
Direct material mix variance	£2,400	F

(h) Direct material yield variance

An input of 45,000 kgs should yield 42,975 kgs (i.e. 95.5% of 45,000 kgs).
(Standard yield of actual input − Actual yield of material input) × Standard material cost

(42,975 kgs − £42,000 kgs) × £3.0157 =	£2,940.3 A*

* Rounded to £2,941 to agree with the equation:

Mix variance ± yield variance = material usage variance
  £2,400 F   £2,941 A   =   £541 A

Section 8

RATIOS

acid test ratio

$$\frac{\text{Quick assets at end of period}}{\text{Current liabilities at end of period}}$$

Measures the ability to pay creditors in the short term. Quick assets comprise cash and those debtors, securities and other assets which can be quickly turned into cash. Also known as the *quick ratio*.

asset cover

$$\frac{\text{Net tangible assets before deducting borrowings (including overdraft)}}{\text{Total borrowings (including overdraft)}}$$

Indicates the safety of the lender's money.

asset value per share

$$\frac{\text{Equity share capital plus reserves}}{\text{Number of issued equity shares}}$$

Shows the value of assets per share, usually for the benefit of equity shareholders.

bad debts ratio

(1) $\dfrac{\text{Bad debts incurred} \times 100}{\text{Turnover on credit}}$

Numerator and denominator should be moving annual totals.

(2) $\dfrac{\text{Bad debts incurred} \times 100}{\text{Total debtors at a point in time}}$

Both ratios highlight the effectiveness of credit control.

capacity ratios

A combination of ratios used to state the relationships between volume levels of production capacity. The more commonly used capacity levels are:

Full capacity – production volume expressed in standard hours that could be achieved if sales orders, supplies and workforce were available for all installed workplaces.

Practical capacity – full capacity less an allowance for known unavoidable volume losses.

Budgeted capacity – standard hours planned for the period, taking into account budgeted sales, supplies and workforce availability.

Idle capacity ratio is then:

$$\frac{\text{Practical capacity standard hours less budgeted standard hours}}{\text{Practical capacity standard hours}}$$

On the following given data, the related ratios are set out below.

Standard hours at full capacity, ideal standard	100
Standard hours at practical capacity, attainable standard	95
Budgeted direct labour (or machine) hours	90
Budgeted standard hours at 90% performance/efficiency	81
Actual direct labour (or machine) hours	85
Standard hours produced	68

Idle capacity ratio $\qquad \dfrac{95 - 81}{95} = 15\%$

Production volume ratio $\qquad \dfrac{68}{81} = 84\%$

Efficiency ratio $\qquad \dfrac{68}{85} = 80\%$

capital turnover

$$\frac{\text{Turnover of the year}}{\text{Average capital employed in year}}$$

Measures the number of times the capital is turned over in the year or alternatively the turnover generated by each £1 of capital employed.

contribution per unit of limiting factor ratio

$$\frac{\text{Contribution (£)}}{\text{Selected limiting factor (units)}}$$

Used in marginal costing to measure the contribution to fixed overhead and profit from a selected limiting factor or other factor.

creditor days ratio

$$\frac{\text{Average trade creditors or at end of period}}{\text{Average daily purchases on credit terms in the period}}$$

Measures the average time taken, in days, to pay for supplies received on credit. This would be based on calendar days. If VAT or other taxes distort the ratio unduly any necessary adjustment should be made.

current ratio

$$\frac{\text{Current assets at end of period}}{\text{Current liabilities at end of period}}$$

An overall test of liquidity.

debtor days ratio

$$\frac{\text{Average trade debtors or at end of period}}{\text{Average daily turnover on credit terms in the period}}$$

Measures the debtors outstanding at the end of the period in terms of average daily sales on credit in the period. This would be based on calendar days. If VAT or other taxes distort the ratio unduly, any necessary adjustment should be made.

Example:
$$\frac{\text{Trade debtors}}{\text{Average daily sales on credit}} = \frac{£50,000}{547} = 91.4 \text{ days}$$

direct hours yield

$$\frac{\text{Direct hours worked} \times 100}{\text{Available hours of direct workers}}$$

Measures the effectiveness with which nominated direct workers are employed on direct work. The alternative expression *efficiency ratio* is not recommended for this ratio.

diverted hours ratio

$$\frac{\text{Diverted hours} \times 100}{\text{Available hours of direct workers}}$$

Highlights the working time of nominated direct workers not spent on direct work.

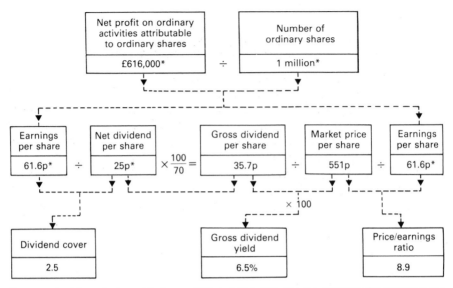

Items marked * can be traced in figures 10.6 and 10.7. See also the definition for 'Earnings per share'.
Net dividend is a term in common usage for an actual dividend paid.
Gross dividend is a term in common usage for an actual dividend paid plus imputed tax (tax credit).

Figure 8.1   Investment ratios

dividend cover

$$\frac{\text{Earnings per share}}{\text{Net dividend per share}}$$

Indicates the number of times the profits attributable to the equity shareholders cover the actual net dividends payable for the period. *See* figure 8.1. Under the present UK tax system earnings per share and dividends per share for this ratio will usually be adjusted for Advanced Corporation Tax (ACT).

dividend per share

$$\frac{\text{Net amount payable to shareholders}}{\text{Number of issued shares ranking for dividend}}$$

Indicates the amount of dividend per share actually payable. Interim and final dividends may be declared separately but for company comparison purposes the dividend per share usually relates to the total dividends per share paid in respect of a financial year.

earnings per share

$$\frac{\text{Attributable equity profit for the period}}{\text{Number of equity shares in issue and ranking for dividend}}$$

SSAP3 defines earnings per share as follows:

The profit in pence attributable to each equity share, based on the consolidated profit of the period after tax and after deducting minority interests and preference dividends, but before taking into account extraordinary items, divided by the number of equity shares in issue and ranking for dividend in respect of the period.

Based on the illustrations in figures 10.6 and 10.7, if there were 1,000,000 issued ordinary shares at the balance sheet date ranking for dividend in respect of the period, then the earning per share would be:

		£000
Profit on ordinary activities after tax		700
Other taxes not shown under the above items	(10)	
Deduct: profit attributable to minorities	(24)	
Deduct: dividends on preference shares	(50)	
	——	(84)
		——
		616
		——

or otherwise, profit available for ordinary shareholders as per figure 10.7 less extraordinary items net of tax.

$$\text{Earnings per share} = \frac{£616,000}{1,000,000} = 61.6 \text{ pence per share}$$

efficiency ratio

$$\frac{\text{Standard hours of production achieved} \times 100}{\text{Actual number of direct working hours}}$$

Measures the efficiency of direct labour.

fixed assets turnover ratio

$$\frac{\text{Turnover of the year}}{\text{Average net book value of fixed assets}}$$

Measures the turnover generated by each £1 of fixed assets, or the number of times fixed assets are turned over in the year.

gearing ratios

Gearing is a term used to described the relationship between shareholders' capital plus reserves, and either prior charge capital or borrowings or both, as follows:

(1) $\dfrac{\text{Prior charge capital (A)}}{\text{Total capital in issue plus reserves (B)}}$

(2) $\dfrac{\text{Total borrowings (C)}}{\text{Total capital in issue plus reserves}}$

(3) $\dfrac{\text{Prior charge capital plus borrowings}}{\text{Total capital in issue plus reserves}}$

(4) $\dfrac{\text{Prior charge capital} \times 100}{\text{Capital employed (D)}}$

Note:

(A) includes preference shares and debentures,

(B) includes prior charge capital plus equity capital and reserves,

(C) comprises total long and short term borrowings,

(D) capital employed could be replaced as a denominator, for management purposes, by prior charge capital plus equity, i.e. excluding such items as minority interests and deferred income.

Ratio 4 above can also be expressed by the formula:

$$\dfrac{\text{Prior charge capital} \times 100}{\text{Equity}}$$

For example:

	£000
Prior charge capital	400
Equity	600
Capital employed	1,000

Then formula 4, example 1

$$\dfrac{\text{Prior charge capital} \times 100}{\text{Capital employed}} = \dfrac{£400 \times 100}{£1,000} = 40\%$$

and formula 4, example 2

$$\dfrac{\text{Prior charge capital} \times 100}{\text{Equity}} = \dfrac{£400 \times 100}{£600} = 66.7\%$$

The company having a high proportion of prior charge capital to equity is *high-geared*, and is *low-geared* if the reverse situation applies. Ratio 4 is often referred to as the *debt ratio*.

gross dividend yield

$$\frac{\text{Actual dividend paid per share plus imputed tax} \times 100}{\text{Market price per share}}$$

Measures the percentage of current share price in terms of gross dividends.

gross profit percentage

$$\frac{\text{Gross profit of the period} \times 100}{\text{Turnover of the period}}$$

A commonly used measure to determine whether selling prices are adequate and to determine selling price policy.

interest cover

$$\frac{\text{Profit before interest and tax}}{\text{All interest payable}}$$

Used by the lender to indicate the vulnerability of the interest payments to a drop in profits.

length of order book

$$\frac{\text{Sales value of orders outstanding}}{\text{Sales value of production per day/week/month}}$$

The sales value of production may be that of, e.g. planned, current or available capacity production. The ratio can also be applied to factored goods by using an appropriate numerator and denominator.

liquidity ratios

A group of measures relating to working capital which indicate the ability to meet liabilities with the assets available.

margin of safety ratio

$$\frac{(\text{Forecast turnover} - \text{breakeven turnover}) \times 100}{\text{Forecast turnover}}$$

Indicates whether forecast turnover is adequate to achieve the breakeven point and by what margin, in order to prompt management action if necessary to improve the turnover or reduce costs.

number of days' stock held

$$\frac{\text{Stock value}}{\text{Average daily cost of sales in period}}$$

Shows the number of days' worth of stock held at the most recent rate of daily turnover. Can be applied to finished stocks, raw materials and work in progress by using appropriate numerators.

number of weeks' stock: finished goods

$$\frac{\text{Finished goods stock}\star}{\text{Average weekly despatches}\star}$$

The number of weeks' stockholding of raw materials, work in progress and finished goods ratios are used internally and measure the efficiency of stock utilisation. Financial analysts who only have access to published accounts often use the total closing stock value in relation to the year's cost of sales.

★ Value or quantity.

Number of weeks' stock: raw materials

$$\frac{\text{Raw materials stock}}{\text{Raw material usage per week}}$$

number of weeks' stock: total stocks

$$\frac{\text{Total stock value}}{\text{Average weekly turnover}}$$

number of weeks' stock: work in progress

$$\frac{\text{Work in progress value}}{\text{Average weekly production value}}$$

price/earnings ratio

$$\frac{\text{Market price of share}}{\text{Earnings per share}}$$

Shows the number of years it would take to recoup the investment in the share out of the earnings attributable. It is a reflection of the market's expectation of future earnings.

production volume ratio

$$\frac{\text{Standard hours of production achieved} \times 100}{\text{Budgeted number of standard hours}}$$

Measures the volume of output compared with budget. The term *activity ratio* is synonymous but is not recommended as the word 'activity' is capable of different interpretation.

profit per employee

$$\frac{\text{Profit before interest payable (or receivable) and tax}}{\text{Average number of employees}}$$

Measures the return obtained from the workforce. Usually expressed per annum. Where there are full and part-time employees an equivalent number of full-time employees is often calculated for this purpose.

profit to turnover ratio (percentage profit on turnover)

$$\frac{\text{Profit before interest and tax} \times 100}{\text{Turnover}}$$

Uses turnover as the measure to determine profit performance. If the numerator is not multiplied by 100 to give a percentage, then it measures the profit generated by each £1 turnover.

Example, based on figure 10.6:

	£
Profit on ordinary activities before tax	1,450
Add back interest payable	50
Profit before interest and tax	1,500

$$\frac{£1,500 \times 100}{£6,600} = 22.7\% \text{ profit to turnover ratio.}$$

rate of return (accounting . . . on investment)

A ratio sometimes used in investment appraisal, which is analogous to the return on capital employed ratio.

Unlike *net present value* and *internal rate of return* the ratio is based on profits as opposed to cash flows. It is represented by the formula:

$$\frac{\text{Average annual profit from the investment} \times 100}{\text{Average investment}}$$

Not a recommended measure.

ratio pyramid
A part of ratio analysis whereby a primary ratio is broken down into secondary ratios which are mathematically linked. For example:

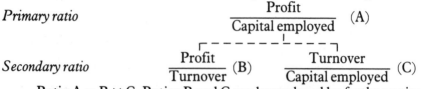

Primary ratio
$$\frac{\text{Profit}}{\text{Capital employed}} \quad (A)$$

Secondary ratio
$$\frac{\text{Profit}}{\text{Turnover}} \ (B) \qquad \frac{\text{Turnover}}{\text{Capital employed}} \ (C)$$

Ratio A = B × C. Ratios B and C can be analysed by further ratios if desired. The pyramid continues with further analysis of the secondary ratios. Examples of extended pyramids are given in figure 8.2.

return on capital employed

$$\frac{\text{Profit before interest and tax}}{\text{Average capital employed in year}}$$

Measures the percentage profit generated as an indication of the productivity of capital employed. In the denominator, the usual average would be that of the capital employed at successive year-ends but problems of seasonality, new capital introduced or other factors, may necessitate taking the average from a greater number of periods within the year. The ratio can be used for different measurement purposes according to constituent parts of average capital employed and definitions of profit. *See* capital employed.

sales per employee

$$\frac{\text{Turnover for the year}}{\text{Average number of employees}}$$

Provides a broad measure of the productivity of the workforce. *See also* profit per employee.

Scheme of ratio analysis for a manufacturing company

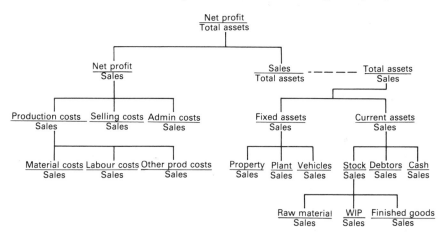

Scheme of ratio analysis for a retail trading company

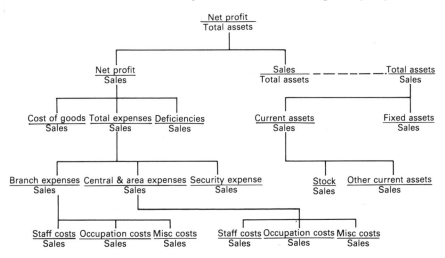

Figure 8.2 Extended ratio pyramids

Section 9

ACCOUNTING DOCUMENTS

advice note
A document prepared to advise a third party in advance of the despatch of goods, usually in quantity only.
Its use as a synonym for delivery note, q.v. is not recommended.

bank reconciliation
A detailed statement reconciling, at a given date, the cash balance in an entity's cash book with that reported by a bank in a bank statement.

Example:

	Cash Book £	Bank £
Balance per bank statement – in credit		2,100
Balance per cash book (overdrawn)	(1,205)	
Cheques drawn but not presented to bank		(4,363)
Cheques received but not credited by bank		1,061
Bank charges not in cash book	(110)	
Dividends collected by bank, not in cash book	113	
Adjusted balances (overdrawn)	(1,202)	(1,202)

bank statement
A record sent at agreed intervals by a bank to its customer setting out all the transactions on his account since the date of the previous statement.

bill
noun – synonym for invoice
verb – to render an account, i.e. to send an invoice or periodic statement.

bill of exchange
An unconditional order in writing, addressed by one person to another, signed by the person giving it, requiring the person to whom it is addressed to pay, on demand or at a fixed or determinable future time, a sum certain in money to or to the order of a specified person, or to bearer (Bills of Exchange Act 1882).

bill of lading
A memorandum prepared by a consignor by which the carrier acknowledges the receipt of goods and which serves as a document of title to the goods consigned.

bill of materials
A specification of the nature and quantity of the materials and parts entering into a particular product.

bill payable
A bill of exchange or promissory note payable, prepared by a drawer to a specified payee and often subject to acceptance by a third party as a guarantor or as a discounter.

bill receivable
A bill of exchange or promissory note receivable.

bin card
A prime entry record of the quantity of stocks, kept on an in/out balance basis, held in designated storage areas.

cash account
A record of receipts and payments in cash, cheques or other forms of payment.

As with other accounts this can be visible or non-visible. Thus the term *cash book* is often used to describe cash accounts which are recorded visibly in book form, and *cash ledger* where the cash accounts are a series of cards or computer records.

certified cheque
A cheque the payment of which is guaranteed by the bank on which it is drawn.

cheque
A bill of exchange drawn on a banker payable on demand (Bills of Exchange Act 1882).

cheque register
A record of original entry of cheques issued or received.

clock card
A document or device which records the starting and finishing time of an employee, e.g. by insertion of a card into a time recording device, for ascertaining total actual attendance time.

It may also be used to record wages payable, and act as a receipt for wages paid. Where an employee also clocks on and off different jobs within his total attendance time, such cards are referred to as job cards.

coin analysis
An analysis of the payroll to show the numbers of different denominations of banknotes and coins required to pay the employees on that payroll.

control account
A total account inserted in a ledger (or section of accounts) to make it self-balancing.
A run of debits and credits is posted to the individual ledger accounts, and the total of both or the net value, is posted to the control account. The balance of the account should thus always equal the total of the balances on the individual accounts in the subsidiary ledger.

cost account
An account recording revenues and expenditures of cost centres or units for control purposes as distinct from the legal requirement of financial reporting.

credit note
A document prepared by the seller notifying the purchaser that his (the purchaser's) account is being reduced by a stated amount because of an allowance, return of goods or cancellation.

current account
A record of transactions between two businesses (usually members of the same group), or between head office and a branch, or between a bank and its customers.

debit note
A document prepared by the purchaser notifying the seller that his (the seller's) account has been reduced by a stated amount because of an allowance, return of goods or cancellation.

delivery note
A document which accompanies goods for delivery and may act as proof of delivery, sometimes referred to as a *consignment note* or a *carrier's note*.

despatch note
A document prepared to advise a third party of actual quantity and date of despatch and method of transportation.

fixed assets register
A record showing details of each item of plant, machinery, fixtures and fittings, and buildings purchased and used by a business. *See* figure 9.1 for an illustration of a manually prepared register.

FIXED ASSETS REGISTER

Machinery/plant/vehicles

Basis: 10 years straight line, no residual value, start end of month following purchase.

Inv date	Inv No.	Asset description	Original cost £	Depreciation														Summary WDV
				1982	83	84	85	86	87	88	89	90	91	92	93	94	
1982		B/F	1,000	1,000	900	800	700	600	500	400	300	200	100	—	—		5,500
4 Apr	103	10 machines type ABC @ £150	1,500	137	150	150	150	150	150	150	150	150	150	13	—		+4,160
25	104	1 Eastman knife	240	18	24	24	24	24	24	24	24	24	24	6			=9,660
7 Sept	105	16 Workplaces @ £120	1,920	96	192	192	192	192	192	192	192	192	192	96			-1,255
20 Nov	106	Compressed air extension	500	4	50	50	50	50	50	50	50	50	50	46			
			4,160	1,255	1,316	1,216	1,116	1,016	916	816	716	616	516	161			8,405
1983																	
10 June	107	5 Air operated presses	3,500		263	350	350	350	350	350	350	350	350	350	87		+4,070
9 Sept	108	1 Felling machine	240		6	24	24	24	24	24	24	24	24	24	18		=12,475
6 Oct	109	3 Flat bed machines	330		—	33	33	33	33	33	33	33	33	33	33		-1,585
			4,070		1,585	1,623	1,523	1,423	1,323	1,223	1,123	1,023	923	568	138		10,890

Note: The register could be extended to show tax allowances taken, current cost information, and cost of repairs and maintenance. In addition, an index should be kept for each asset showing location, identifying number, purchase date, supplier, invoice number, cost and depreciation class.

Figure 9.1 Fixed assets register

goods received note
A document prepared by a recipient to record receipt of goods either (i) because an advice note has not been received, or (ii) to create a common format for use within the recipient's system.

intra-group account
A record of transactions between two companies in the same group.

invoice
A document prepared by a supplier showing the description, quantities, price and value of goods delivered, or services performed.

To the supplier this is a sales invoice; to the purchaser the same document is a purchase invoice. The invoice may also state terms of payment.

invoice register
A list of purchase invoices recording date of receipt of the invoice, the supplier, invoice value and to whom the invoice has been passed, to ensure that all invoices received are processed by the accounting system.

job card/sheet
A document which records time spent on a job and/or materials used.

It may also record the cost of the labour and materials used on that job and overheads charged to it.

journal
A record of financial transactions, such as transfers between accounts and correction of book-keeping errors.

labour transfer note
A document which records the transfer of labour from one cost centre to another, or from one cost unit to another.

ledger
A collective term for a number of accounts, e.g. several sales accounts constitute a sales ledger.

A ledger can either be visible, e.g. a binder holding visible record accounts or non-visible, i.e. in a computer.

letter of credit
A letter or document issued by a bank on behalf of a customer authorising the person named therein to draw money to a specified amount from its branches or correspondents, usually overseas, when the conditions set out in the document have been met.

lost time record
A document recording the number of hours that a machine or employee is *not* producing, with reasons, and if possible, responsibilities.

Lost time can include, for example, waiting time and maintenance.

machine time record
A document which records the amount of time a machine is operated or not operated.

It may also record the cost of the time and details of the production achieved.

materials returned note
A document which records the return of unused material to store.

materials/stores requisition
A document which requests, and when approved, authorises the issue of a specified quantity of materials.

It may initiate entry in materials/stores ledgers.

materials transfer note
A document which records the transfer of material from one store to another, from one cost centre to another, or from one cost unit to another, usually in both quantity and value.

nominal account
A record of revenues and expenditures, liabilities and assets classified by their nature, e.g. sales, rent, rates, electricity, wages, share capital.

These are sometimes referred to as impersonal accounts but the term nominal account is preferred. These accounts can be extended by coding to produce historical information for control purposes, e.g. to compare with planned costs, and to control expenditure by cost centres.

Illustration:

Code 6.0 *Power, light and heat*

		Factory location		
		A	B	C
6.1	Electricity	6.1.1	6.1.2	6.1.3
6.2	Oil	6.2.1	6.2.2	6.2.3
6.3	Gas	6.3.1	6.3.2	6.3.3

out-of-date cheque
A cheque which has not been presented to the bank on which it is drawn for payment within a reasonable time of its date (six months in the UK) and which may therefore be dishonoured by the bank without any breach of the banker–customer contract.

paid-cheque
A cheque which has been honoured by the bank on which it was drawn, and bears evidence of payment on its face.

payroll
A record showing the gross wages or salaries earned by each employee for defined periods, and deductions, e.g. for income tax and national insurance, to arrive at net pay.

It may also include details of the employer's associated employment costs.

payroll analysis
An analysis of a payroll for cost accounting purposes. This may include:
1. gross wages per department or operation,
2. gross wages per labour classification,
3. gross wages by product,
4. an analysis of the constituent parts of gross wages, e.g. direct wages and lost time.

The term wages abstract is not recommended. Not to be confused with coin analysis, *see* page 104.

personal account
A record of amounts receivable from or payable to a person or an entity.

A collection of these accounts is known as a sales/debtors ledger, or a purchases/creditors ledger. The terms sales and purchase ledgers are preferred. In the USA the terms *receivables ledger* and *payables ledger* are used.

petty cash account
A record of relatively small cash receipts and payments, usually kept under separate control and involving the holding and disbursement of small cash sums.

petty cash voucher
A document showing expenditure of petty cash, usually requiring the attachment of receipted invoices, with authorising and receiving signatures.

pro-forma invoice
An invoice sent to the purchaser in advance of goods, for completion of business formalities (usually for payment before goods are despatched).

promissory note

An unconditional promise in writing made by one person to another, signed by the maker, engaging to pay on demand or at a fixed or determinable future time, a sum certain in money to or to the order of a specified person or to bearer (Bills of Exchange Act 1882).

purchase contract/sales contract

A contract between two or more parties for the purchase/sale of goods on agreed terms.

purchase order

A document ordering goods or services from a supplier, specifying quantities, price, delivery dates and terms for a purchase contract.

purchase requisition

A document, for example from a stores to a buying office, requesting the purchase of goods or services, and usually:
1. stating the quantity and description of goods to be purchased or services to be supplied, and
2. indenting and, when authorised, calling for a purchase order.

sales order

A document issued by a supplier as an acknowledgement of a purchase order, which may over-ride the buyer's detailed purchase terms.

sight draft

A bill of exchange payable at sight, i.e. on demand or presentation, but with respect to which three days of grace are allowed for payment.

standing order

1. In banking: a customer's authority to his bank whereby he authorises the bank to pay a stated amount to another person at specified dates.
2. An order issued as authority for the production or purchase of goods or services, as need or opportunity arises, usually limited by a stated maximum.

time sheet

A document which records time in relation to an employee.

This may be total time attended, time spent on specific activities, waiting and other non-working time, e.g. holidays and sickness; it may also be used to record wages payable.

voucher

Any documentary evidence in support of an accounting entry.

CASH FLOW STATEMENT – RECEIPTS AND PAYMENTS METHOD

		£000
Bank overdraft at beginning		−500
Receipts		
payments by debtors	200	
investment income (net)	100	
	——	
		+300
Payments		
materials and services	80	
wages and salaries – net	40	
wages and salaries – NI and PAYE	10	
capital items	20	
interest payable (not accrued)	10	
corporation tax payable	5	
dividends payable	20	
	——	
		−185
Overdraft at end		−385

CASH FLOW STATEMENT – BALANCE SHEET METHOD

Bank overdraft at beginning		−500
Inflow		
Profit before tax	80	
Depreciation	20	
Investment income	130	
Reduction in debtors	20	
Increase in creditors	5	
	——	
		+255
Outflow		
Increase in stocks	20	
Capital expenditure	40	
Interest chargeable	20	
Corporation tax	40	
Dividends	20	
	——	
		−140
Overdraft at end		−385

Figure 10.1   Cash flow statement

Section 10

ACCOUNTS, STATEMENTS AND REPORTS

account sales

A statement rendered to a consignor of merchandise by the consignee giving particulars such as the sales of the consigned merchandise, amount of any such merchandise remaining unsold, gross proceeds, expenses incurred by the consignee, consignee's commission, and net amount due to the consignor.

annual report and accounts

A set of statements comprising a management report (in the case of companies the directors' report), the balance sheet, profit and loss account or other revenue account, and related notes.

Consolidated or group accounts are included if applicable.

audit report

1. A report by an auditor in accordance with his terms of appointment.
2. The formal document in which an auditor expresses his opinion as to whether, in accordance with accepted accountancy principles and legal requirements, the financial statements of an entity show a true and fair view of:

(a) its position at a given date, and

(b) the results of its operations for the accounting period ended on that date.

balance sheet

A statement of the financial position of an entity at a given date disclosing the value of the assets, liabilities and accumulated funds such as shareholders' contributions and reserves, prepared to give a true and fair view of the state of the entity at that date.

Figure 10.9 shows a specimen balance sheet. In the case of certain limited liability companies the format of the balance sheet is specified in the Companies Act.

branch accounts

A term used for a form of departmental accounts where different geographical locations are involved; usually applied in retail businesses and also to branches in other countries where the branches are not incorporated.

cash flow statement

A statement produced for the management of an entity showing, by broad category, the cash received and spent for a given period.

It may also include a forecast for future periods. This should not be confused with the Source and Application of Funds Statement which reconciles the profit declared with the net change in cash. There are two main methods of preparing cash flow statements, being the receipt and payments method and the balance sheet method. *See* figure 10.1.

consolidated financial statements/group accounts

A form of group accounts which presents the information contained in the separate financial statements of a holding company and its subsidiaries as if they were the accounts of a single entity (SSAP 14).
Notes
1. Only transactions with those outside the entity are reflected in the consolidated accounts, inter-company transactions and their profit content being eliminated.
2. Assets, liabilities, revenues and expenses of the subsidiaries are combined with those of the parent company.
3. All reciprocal accounts are eliminated, the precise method being dependent upon the way in which the parent company reflects its investment in subsidiaries.

credit report

A report giving information about an individual or corporation which may bear on a decision to grant credit to that individual or corporation.

current cost accounting statements

Annual financial statements prepared in accordance with Statement of Standard Accounting Practice No. 16.

The current cost accounts (CCA) contain a profit and loss account, and a balance sheet in which assets and liabilities are included, as far as practicable, on the following bases:
(a) Land and buildings, plant and machinery, and stocks which are subject to a cost of sales adjustment, at their value to the business.
(b) Investments in associated companies: either at the applicable proportion of the associated companies' net assets stated under the standard or, where such information is not readily available, at directors' best estimate thereof.
(c) Other investments (excluding those treated as current assets) at directors' valuation. Where the investment is listed and the directors' valuation is materially different from midmarket value, the basis of valuation and the reasons for the difference should be stated.

Y Limited and Subsidiaries

**Group current cost profit and loss account
for the year ended 31st December 1980**

	1979 £000	1979 £000	1980 £000	1980 £000
Turnover		18,000		20,000
Profit before interest and taxation on the historical cost basis	2,420		2,900	
Less: Current cost operating adjustments	1,320		1,510	
Current cost operating profit	1,100		1,390	
Gearing adjustment	(170)		(166)	
Interest payable less receivable	180		200	
		10		34
Current cost profit before taxation		1,090		1,356
Taxation		610		730
Current cost profit attributable to shareholders		480		626
Dividends		400		430
Retained current cost profit of the year		80		196
Current cost earnings per share		16.0p		20.9p
Operating profit return on the average of the net operating assets		5.2%		6.0%

Statement of retained profits/reserves

	1979 £000	1980 £000
Retained current cost profit of the year	80	196
Movements on current cost reserve	1,850	2,054
Movements on other reserves	NIL	NIL
	1,930	2,250
Retained profits/reserves at the beginning of the year	14,150	16,080
Retained profits/reserves at the end of the year	16,080	18,330

Where applicable, minority interests and extraordinary items should be presented in a manner consistent with the historical cost accounts

Y Limited and Subsidiaries

**Summarised group current cost balance sheet
as at 31st December 1980**

	1979 £000	1979 £000	1980 £000	1980 £000
Assets employed:				
Fixed assets		18,130		19,530
Net current assets:				
Stock	3,200		4,000	
Monetary working capital	700		800	
Total working capital	3,900		4,800	
Proposed dividends	(400)		(430)	
Other current liabilities (Net)	(600)		(570)	
		2,900		3,800
		21,030		23,330
Financed by:				
Share capital and reserves:				
Share capital	3,000		3,000	
Current cost reserve	12,350		14,404	
Other reserves and retained profit	3,730		3,926	
		19,080		21,330
Loan capital		1,950		2,000
		21,030		23,330

Figure 10.2 Current cost accounting statements

(d) Intangible assets (excluding goodwill) at the best estimate of their value to the business.
(e) Goodwill (premium or discount) as per historical cost accounts.
(f) Current assets, other than stocks subject to a cost of sales adjustment: on the historical cost basis.
(g) All liabilities: on the historical cost basis.

See figure 10.2 for an example of a CCA profit and loss account and balance sheet.

DEBTORS' AGE ANALYSIS							PREPARED AT . . . . .19. . . .
Name of debtor	Total debt			Age			Comments
		1 month	2 months	3 months	4 months	older	
A Limited	25,232	12,000	13,232				
B Limited	15,000		5,000	(a) 10,000			(a) deliveries stopped sales dept visiting.
C Limited	5,643					(b) 5,643	(b) delivery under query with sales dept.
D Limited	100,000	20,000	80,000				
X Limited	1,263					(c) 1,263	(c) under litigation
Y Limited	150,463	102,000	(e) 30,000	(d) 18,463			(d) rejections being investigated
Z Limited	3,470	3,470					(e) 20,000 since received.
TOTAL £	501,232	187,470	278,393	28,463	—	6,906	

General comment 1 The bulk of debtors are in the two months column. This needs to be watched to make sure they do not slip into the 3 months column.
2 Company D needs to be chased, and further deliveries held if payment not quickly received.

Figure 10.3 Debtors' age analysis

debtors' age analysis

An analysis of sums owing by debtors, classified according to age of debt. See figure 10.3.

deficiency (or surplus) account
A statement in a prescribed form, which shows the excess, if any, of liabilities over assets (or vice versa) at a given date.
The account shows how the debtor has arrived at his present position. The balance on this account, either a surplus or a deficiency, must agree with that shown on the statement of affairs.

departmental accounts
Accounts which show the revenue and expenditure of the various departments of an entity for a given period.
They may take the form of a trading and profit and loss account for each department but could also be an operating account for a service department.

financial statements
Summaries from accounts to provide information for interested parties.
The most common financial statements are:
- trading and profit and loss account,
- profit and loss appropriation account,
- balance sheet, and the
- source and application of funds statement.

Figures 4.1 and 10.5 illustrate the relationship of the trading, profit and loss, and profit and loss appropriation accounts compiled on alternative bases.

fixed asset statement
A statement showing the value of fixed assets held at the beginning of an accounting period, acquisitions and disposals during the period, depreciation, and the value at the end of the period. *See* figure 10.10.

income and expenditure account
An account (used by concerns such as clubs, associations, or charities, whose main objective is not profit-making) which shows the excess of income over expenditure (or vice versa) for a given period.
The account is similar to a profit and loss account, and is usually accompanied by a balance sheet.

profit and loss appropriation account
An extension of the trading and profit and loss account which shows how the net profit, after taxation, has been appropriated to dividends and minorities and shows the profit retained. *See* figure 10.5.

receipts and payments account
An account which shows in summarised form the cash transactions during a given period.

GROUPS LIMITED

STATEMENT OF SOURCE AND APPLICATION OF FUNDS
(based on the accounts of the Group and
showing the effects of acquiring a subsidiary on
the separate assets and liabilities of the Group).

	This Year			Last Year		
	£'000	£'000	£'000	£'000	£'000	£'000
Source of funds						
Profit before tax and extraordinary items, less						
minority interests			2,025			2,610
Extraordinary items			450			(170)
			2,475			2,440
Adjustments for items not involving the movement of funds:						
Minority interests in the retained profits of						
the year			25			30
Depreciation			345			295
Profits retained in associated companies			(40)			—
Total generated from operations			2,805			2,765
Funds from other sources						
Shares issued in part consideration of the						
acquisition of subsidiary★			290			—
Capital raised under executive option scheme			100			80
			3,195			2,845
Application of funds						
Dividends paid		(650)			(650)	
Tax paid		(770)			(970)	
Purchase of fixed assets★		(660)			(736)	
Purchase of goodwill on acquisition of subsidiary★		(30)			—	
Debentures redeemed		(890)			—	
			(3,000)			(2,356)
			195			489
Increase/decrease in working capital						
Increase in stocks★		120			166	
Increase in debtors★		100			122	
Decrease in creditors – excluding taxation and						
proposed dividends★		75			17	
Movement in net liquid funds:						
Increase (decrease) in cash balance★	(35)			10		
Increase (decrease) in short-term investments	(65)			174		
		(100)			184	
			195			489

★SUMMARY OF THE EFFECTS OF THE ACQUISITION OF SUBSIDIARY LIMITED

Net assets acquired		*Discharged by*	
Fixed assets	290	Shares issued	290
Goodwill	30	Cash paid	60
Stocks	40		
Debtors	30		
Creditors	(40)		
	350		350

Figure 10.4 Source and application of funds

It includes the opening and closing balances of cash in hand and/or at the bank. Receipts are shown on the debit side and payments on the credit side.

The main differences between this and the income and expenditure account are:

Receipts and payments account	*Income and expenditure account*
Includes cash transactions only	Includes accruals and prepayments
Includes capital receipts and capital payments	Excludes capital receipts and capital payments
Balance represents cash in hand, bank balance, or bank overdraft at a particular date.	Balance represents surplus/ deficiency of income over expenditure for a given period.

source and application of funds statement
A statement showing the sources and values of funds flowing into an entity, the way in which they have been used and how any net surplus or deficiency in short and long term funds has been applied.

It provides a link between the balance sheet at the beginning of the period, the profit and loss account for the period, and the balance sheet at the end of the period and forms part of the audited accounts of a company.

The example, figure 10.4, is format 2 from SSAP 10, used for groups with subsidiary companies.

statement
A shortened form of 'statement of account', listing sums due, usually as a list of specified unpaid invoices from a supplier to a purchaser, items paid on account but not offset against particular invoices, credit notes, debit notes and discounts.

statement of affairs
A statement in a prescribed form, showing the estimated financial position of a debtor or of a company which may be unable to meet its debts.

It contains a summary of the debtor's total assets and liabilities. The assets are shown at their estimated realisable values. The various classes of creditors, such as preferential, secured, partly secured and unsecured, are shown separately. Usually prepared by a Receiver.

suspense account
An account in which debits or credits are held temporarily until sufficient information is available for them to be posted to the correct accounts.

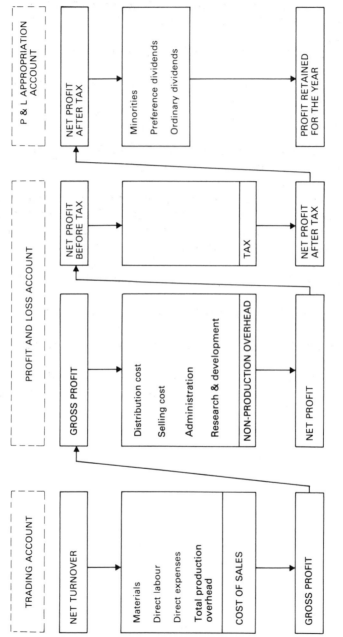

Figure 10.5 Trading and profit and loss account using absorption costing
(*See* figure 4.1 for marginal costing)

The reasons for posting an amount to a suspense account are:
1. inadequate information on the treatment of one or both sides of a transaction,
2. errors in coding or in the value to be posted on one side of a transaction,
3. to accommodate the difference in the two sides of the trial balance, to enable accounts to be drawn up.

trading and profit and loss account

(a) *Trading account*
An account which shows the gross profit/loss or contribution generated by an entity for a given period.

(b) *Profit and loss account*
An account beginning with gross profit/loss or contribution which, after adding other income and deducting various expenses shows the profit or loss on the ordinary activities of the business. Figure 10.6 shows a typical format which meets the requirements of the Companies Act and the definitions which follow are related to that format. However reference should be made to the four alternative formats in the Act.

In some cases small entities may combine the two accounts.

trial balance

A list of the debit and credit balances on the accounts, extracted at a given date.

If the records have been correctly maintained under the double entry system the total of the debit balances will equal the total of the credit balances.

PROFIT AND LOSS ACCOUNT FOR THE YEAR ENDED 31 DECEMBER xxxx

		£000
Turnover		6,600
Opening stock	1,200	
Direct materials and components	1,500	
Direct wages	1,550	
	4,250	
Less: closing stock	1,400	
Direct cost of sales	2,850	
Overhead		
Indirect wages and salaries	900	
National insurance	240	
Company pension scheme	50	
Canteen subsidy	80	
Power, light, heat	200	
Rent and rates	100	
Insurance	60	
Depreciation	200	
Other costs (listed separately as appropriate)	645	
Total overhead	2,475	
Less: transferred to distribution, selling, publicity, administration, research and development	(825)	
Factory overhead	1,650	
Cost of sales		4,500
Gross profit		2,100
Distribution cost	(200)	
Selling cost	(150)	
Publicity	(50)	
Administration cost	(300)	
Research and Development cost	(125)	
Other operating income	100	
Income from shares in group companies	35	
Income from shares in related companies	65	
Income from other fixed asset investments	25	
Other interest receivable and similar income	20	
Amounts written off investments	(20)	
Interest payable	(50)	
		(650)
Profit on ordinary activities before tax		1,450
Tax on profit or loss on ordinary activities		(750)
Profit or loss on ordinary activities after taxation		700
Extraordinary income	270	
Extraordinary charges	(200)	
Extraordinary profit or (loss)	70	
Tax on extraordinary profit or loss	(36)	
		34
Other taxes not shown under the above items		(10)
Profit for the financial year (to appropriation account)		724

Figure 10.6 Profit and loss account

Note: Figures 10.6, 10.7, 10.8 and 10.9 are illustrative only. Comparative amounts must normally be given.

PROFIT AND LOSS APPROPRIATION ACCOUNT FOR THE YEAR ENDED 31 DECEMBER xxxx

		£000
Profit for the financial year (*see* Fig. 10.6)		724
Less:		
Profit attributable to minorities	24	
Dividends on preference shares	50	
	—	
		74
		—
Profit available for ordinary shareholders		650
Dividends on ordinary shares		250
		—
Profit retained for the year		400
		—

Figure 10.7 Profit and loss appropriation account

STATEMENT OF RETAINED PROFITS/RESERVES FOR THE YEAR ENDING 31 DECEMBER xxxx

		£000
Profit retained for the year		400
Retained profits/reserves at beginning of year as previously reported	969	
Prior year adjustment (see note 1)	80	
	—	
As restated		889
		—
Retained profits/reserves at end of year		1,289
		—

Note
Published accounts should explain the reason for the prior year adjustment, together with its effect on previously published profit and loss accounts and balance sheets. For a detailed example *see* SSAP 6.

Figure 10.8 Prior year adjustment

BALANCE SHEET, AS AT 31 DECEMBER xxxx		
	£000	£000
Fixed assets		
Intangible Assets		
Development costs	35	
Goodwill	225	
	—	260
Tangible Assets		
Land and buildings	201	
Plant, machinery, fixtures, fittings	785	
Vehicles	50	
	—	1,036
Long term investments		
Shares in group companies	400	
Loans to group companies	100	
Shares in related companies	50	
Investments	500	
	—	1,050
Current assets:		
Stocks	1,094	
Debtors	1,288	
Amounts owed by group companies	250	
Short term investments	535	
Cash at bank and in hand	106	
	3,273	
Creditors: amounts falling due within one year	652	
Net current assets (liabilities)		2,621
TOTAL ASSETS LESS CURRENT LIABILITIES		4,967
REPRESENTED BY:		
Creditors: amounts falling due after more than one year		
Debenture loans	200	
Bank loans and overdrafts	900	
Trade creditors	78	
Amounts owed to group companies	400	
Taxation	150	
		1,728
Provision for defe.red taxation		600
Capital and reserves:		
Issued share capital	1,000	
Share premium account	150	
Revaluation reserve	200	
Profit and loss account	1,289	
		2,639
CAPITAL EMPLOYED		4,967

Figure 10.9   Balance sheet

	Land and buildings £000			Plant and equipment £000			Total £000
	Cost or as revalued	Depreciation	Net book value	Cost or as revalued	Depreciation	Net book value	Net book value
GROUP							
At beginning of year	804	283	521	4,000	1,770	2,230	2,751
Exchange adjustments	(49)	(16)	(33)	(148)	(61)	(87)	(120)
Capital expenditure	71		71	653		653	724
Revaluations	18	(18)	36	(39)	(104)	65	101
Disposals	(11)	(5)	(6)	(100)	(77)	(23)	(29)
Depreciation for year		30	(30)		301	(301)	(331)
At end of year	833	274	559	4,366	1,829	2,537	3,096
COMPANY							
At beginning of year	290	137	153	2,360	1,134	1,226	1,379
Capital expenditure	28		28	285		285	313
Disposals	(4)	(1)	(3)	(34)	(32)	(2)	(5)
Depreciation for year		13	(13)		167	(167)	(180)
At end of year	314	149	165	2,611	1,269	1,342	1,507

Figure 10.10   Fixed asset statement

Section 11

INCOME AND EXPENDITURE

accrued expenses
Costs relating to a period which have not so far been taken into account because they have not yet been invoiced by the supplier or paid.
A common example is electricity, where the supplying corporation invoices for consumption in arrears.

administration cost
Cost of management, and of secretarial, accounting and administrative services, which cannot be directly related to the production, marketing, research or development functions of the enterprise.

appraisal costs (quality)
The costs of assessing quality achieved.
The costs include those of the following functions: laboratory acceptance testing, inspection and test (including goods inwards), in-process inspection, set-up for inspection and test, inspection and test materials, product quality audits, review of test and inspection data, field (on-site) performance testing, internal testing and release, evaluation of site materials and spare parts, and data processing of inspection and test reports (BS 6143).

attributable profit (on contracts)
That part of the total profit currently estimated to arise over the duration of the contract (after allowing for likely increases in costs so far as not recoverable under the terms of the contract) which fairly reflects the profit attributable to that part of the work performed at the accounting date. (There can be no attributable profit until the outcome of the contract can be assessed with reasonable certainty). (SSAP 9).

bad debt
A debt which is, or is considered to be, uncollectable and is, therefore, written off as a charge to the profit and loss account.

bank charge
An amount charged by a bank to its customer for services provided, e.g. for operating current accounts, arranging foreign currency transactions or letters of credit, but excluding interest and discount.

capital expenditure
Expenditure on fixed assets or additions thereto intended to benefit future accounting periods (in contrast to revenue expenditure which

benefits a current period) or expenditure which increases the capacity, efficiency, life span or economy of operation of an existing fixed asset.

cost of sales
The sum of direct cost of sales plus factory overhead attributable to the turnover.

In management accounts this may be referred to as *production cost of sales*, or *cost of goods sold*.

current cost operating profit
The surplus arising from the ordinary activities of the business in the period after allowing for the impact of price changes on the funds needed to continue the existing business and maintain its operating capability, whether financed by share capital or borrowing.

It is calculated before interest on net borrowing and taxation. Three adjustments to trading profits, calculated on the historical cost basis before interest, are required to arrive at current cost operating profit. These are called the depreciation, cost of sales and monetary working capital adjustments (SSAP 16).

current cost profit attributable to shareholders
The surplus for the period after allowing for the impact of price changes on the funds needed to maintain the shareholders' proportion of the operating capability.

It is calculated after interest, taxation and extraordinary items (SSAP 16).

depreciation
The measure of the wearing out, consumption or other loss of value of a fixed asset whether arising from use, effluxion of time or obsolescence through technology and market changes (SSAP 12).

depreciation adjustment
The difference between the value to the business of the part of fixed assets consumed during the accounting period and the amount of depreciation charged on an historical cost basis.

The resulting total depreciation charge thus represents the value to the business of the part of fixed assets consumed in earning the revenue of the period (SSAP 16).

development cost
The cost of using scientific or technical knowledge in order to produce new or substantially improved materials, devices, products, processes, systems or services prior to the commencement of commercial production (SSAP 13).

direct cost of sales

The sum of direct materials consumed, direct wages, direct expenses and variable production overhead.

In management accounts this may be referred to as *direct production cost of sales. See* figure 10.6.

direct expenses

Costs other than materials or labour, which can be identified in a specific product or saleable service.

direct labour cost

The cost of remuneration for employees' efforts and skills applied directly to a product or saleable service and which can be identified separately in product costs.

direct materials cost

The cost of materials entering into and becoming constituent elements of a product or saleable service and which can be identified separately in product cost.

distribution cost

Cost incurred in warehousing saleable products and in delivering products to customers.

dividend

A distribution to shareholders out of profits, usually in the form of cash.

employment costs

A generic term given to costs attributable to an employee, in addition to gross wages/salaries.

They usually include employers' national health insurance and state pensions contributions, employers' pension premiums, holidays with pay, employers' contributions to sickness benefit schemes and other benefits, e.g. protective clothing and canteen subsidies.

energy cost

The amount spent on electricity, gas, coal, oil, petrol or other form of consumable energy for an entity's own use in for example, production, transportation, heating, cooling or ventilating.

exceptional items

Items of an abnormal size and incidence which are derived from the ordinary activities of the business, and therefore require separate disclosure (SSAP 6).

They are taken into account in arriving at the profit or loss on ordinary activities before tax.

external failure costs (quality)
Costs arising outside the manufacturing organisation of failure to achieve specified quality (after transfer of ownership to the customer). The costs include:
complaints administration, product or customer service including product liability costs, the costs of handling and accounting for rejected products including recall and retrofit costs, the costs of analysing and repairing materials returned by customers, warranty replacement, the costs arising from replacing products due to marketing errors, design and specification errors and factory or installation errors (BS 6143).

extraordinary income and charges
Income or cost which derives from events or transactions outside the ordinary activities of the business and which are both material and expected not to occur frequently or regularly.

They do not include items which, though exceptional on account of size and incidence (and which may therefore require separate disclosure), derive from the ordinary activities of the business. Neither do they include prior year items merely because they relate to a prior year (SSAP 6 – Revised).

fixed overhead cost
The cost which accrues in relation to the passage of time and which, within certain output and turnover limits, tends to be unaffected by fluctuations in the levels of activity (output or turnover).

Examples are rent, rates, insurance and executive salaries. Other terms used include *period cost* and *policy cost*.

gearing adjustment
The adjustment required to the current cost operating profit to determine (after also allowing for interest payable/receivable and taxation) the current cost profit attributable to shareholders, where a proportion of the net operating assets is financed by net borrowing (SSAP 16).

gross profit
Turnover less cost of sales. *See* figure 10.5.

income from shares in group companies
Dividends received or receivable from companies whose results are consolidated into the group accounts.

income from shares in related companies
Dividends received from related companies.

Related companies are defined in the Companies Act as any body corporate in which the reporting enterprise holds directly or indirectly on a long term basis a qualifying capital interest for the purpose of securing a contribution to the enterprise's own activities by the exercise of any control or influence arising from that interest.

In this context qualifying capital interest means an interest in shares comprised in the equity share capital of the body corporate, where the nominal value of the relevant shares held by the reporting enterprise is equal to twenty per cent or more of the nominal value of all relevant shares in the body corporate. *See also* paragraph 91 of the 8th Schedule to the Companies Act 1948.

Reporting enterprise means any body corporate, including where appropriate its subsidiaries, which prepares and presents its accounts in compliance with the 8th Schedule to the Companies Act 1948.

indirect expenses
Expenses which are not charged directly to a product, e.g. buildings insurance, water rates.

indirect labour cost
Labour costs which are not charged directly to a product, e.g. supervision.

indirect materials cost
Materials costs which are not charged directly to a product, e.g. coolants, cleaning materials.

interest payable
Interest paid or payable for the year, including that on bank overdrafts and long term loans.

The Companies Act states that amounts payable to group companies shall be stated separately.

internal failure costs (quality)
Costs arising within the organisation of failure to achieve the quality specified.

In a manufacturing company these may include defect/failure analysis, re-inspection and testing, the losses incurred due to the failure of purchased items to meet specification, reviewing product designs and specifications, and losses due to non-conformance leading to reduced selling prices (BS 6143).

marketing cost
The cost incurred in researching the potential markets and promoting products in suitably attractive forms and at acceptable prices.

minority interest
Shares held in a subsidiary company by members other than the holding company or its nominees plus the appropriate portion of the accumulated reserves (including share premium account).

monetary working capital adjustment (MWCA)
An adjustment in respect of monetary working capital when determining current cost operating profit.

This adjustment should represent the amount of additional (or reduced) finance needed for monetary working capital as a result of changes in the input price of goods and services used and financed by the business (SSAP 16).

obsolescence
The measure of the loss of value of a fixed asset due to advances in technology or changes in market conditions for the product.

overhead cost
The total cost of indirect materials, indirect labour and indirect expenses.

Note: The synonymous term *burden* is in common use in the USA and in subsidiaries of American companies in the UK.

prevention costs (quality)
The cost of any action taken to investigate, prevent or reduce defects and failures.

The costs include those of the following functions:
quality engineering, design and development of quality control and measurement equipment, quality planning activities by functions other than quality assurance, calibration and maintenance of production equipment used to evaluate quality, the maintenance and calibration of test and inspection equipment used in control of quality, supplier assurance, quality training and the administration and audit of quality (BS 6143).

prime cost
The total cost of direct materials, direct labour and direct expenses.

The term prime cost is commonly restricted to direct production costs only and so does not customarily include direct costs of marketing or research and development.

prior year adjustments
Material adjustments applicable to prior years arising from changes in accounting policies and from the correction of fundamental errors.

They do not include the normal recurring corrections and adjustments of accounting estimates made in prior years. A statement of retained profit/reserves showing any prior year adjustments should immediately follow the profit and loss account for the year (SSAP 6 – Revised). *See* figure 10.8.

production cost
Prime cost plus absorbed production overhead.

profit attributable to minorities
That part of the profit for the financial year which is attributable to shareholders in subsidiary companies who are not the holding company or its nominees.

profit available for ordinary shareholders
The residue of profit for the financial year, attributable to the ordinary shareholders of the company, after all prior charge capital has been serviced.

profit or loss for the financial year
The total of profit or loss on ordinary activities after tax plus or minus extraordinary income or charges net of tax, and net of any other taxes not shown elsewhere.

profit or loss on ordinary activities before tax
The profit or loss before taking into account taxation and extraordinary gains or charges, but after charging exceptional items.

profit or loss on ordinary activities after tax
The profit or loss on ordinary activities before tax, less taxation attributable to that profit or loss.

publicity cost
(a) Cost incurred in advertising and promotion as aids to the eventual sales of goods or services.
(b) Cost incurred in advertising and promotion of an entity as distinct from its products or services (public relations).

quality related costs
The expenditure incurred in defect prevention and appraisal activities and the losses due to internal and external failure of a product or service, through failure to meet agreed specification. Quality costs are classified as:
prevention cost,
appraisal cost,
internal failure cost,
external failure cost.

research cost (applied)
The cost of original investigation undertaken in order to gain new scientific or technical knowledge and directed towards a specific practical aim or objective (SSAP 13).

research cost (basic)
The cost of original investigation undertaken in order to gain new scientific or technical knowledge and understanding, not primarily directed towards any specific practical aim or application (SSAP 13).

revenue expenditure
Expenditure on the supply and manufacture of goods and provision of services charged in the accounting period in which they are consumed.

This includes repairs and depreciation of fixed assets as distinct from the provision of those assets. *See* Capital expenditure.

selling cost
Cost incurred in securing orders, usually including salesmens' salaries, commissions and travelling expenses. *See* marketing cost.

turnover
Amounts derived from the provision of goods and services falling within the company's ordinary activities, after deduction of trade discounts, value added tax, and any other taxes based on the amounts so derived (Companies Act).

This would normally be invoiced sales less returns and allowances.

Section 12

ASSETS AND LIABILITIES

asset
Any possession of value.

back-to-back loan
A form of financing whereby money borrowed in one country or currency is covered by the lending of an equivalent amount in another.

bank overdraft
A borrowing from a bank on current account, usually repayable on demand.

The maximum is agreed beforehand with the bank, and interest accrues on a daily basis. The customer only pays interest on the amount borrowed and not on the total borrowing facility available to him.

bonus or scrip issue
The capitalisation of the reserves of a company by the issue of bonus shares to existing shareholders, in proportion to their holdings, such shares being normally fully paid-up with no monetary payments being made.

capital commitment
(a) The aggregate amount or estimated amount of contracts for capital expenditure, so far as not provided for; and
(b) the aggregate amount or estimated amount of capital expenditure authorised by the directors which has not been contracted for (Companies Act).

capital employed
The funds used by an entity for its operations.

This can be expressed at various levels according to purpose of use. For evaluating shareholders' capital employed for example, sums paid for goodwill out of shareholders' resources by management must be included. However it may be irrelevant for the professional management of a subsidiary that a premium was paid on the original purchase price many years ago, or that a high interest burden arises from past positions, because the manager can only be held responsible for the tangible assets within his control. The distinction can be drawn as follows:

	£000	
Fixed assets	—	
Investments	—	
Working capital		
Stock	—	
Trade debtors and prepayments	—	
Short term cash	—	
Less trade creditors and accruals	(—)	
Operations management capital employed	—	A
Less: tax creditor	(—)	
Less: dividends payable	(—)	
Company capital employed	—	B
Less: borrowings	(—)	
Plus: goodwill	—	
Shareholders' capital employed	—	C
Financed by:		
Share capital	—	
Reserves	—	
	—	

A and B to be related to pre-tax and pre-interest profits.
C to be related to profits after tax.
Where there are minority interests and deferred items, they would usually be included in B but excluded from C.

contingent liabilities
Liabilities which are dependent on a condition which exists at the balance sheet date, where the outcome will be confirmed only on the occurrence or non-occurrence of one or more uncertain future events (SSAP 18).

convertible loan stock
A loan which gives the holder the right to convert to other securities, normally ordinary shares, at a predetermined rate and time.

creditor
A person or an entity to whom money is owed.

creditors or accounts payable (in a balance sheet)
Money owed to suppliers or others.

cumulative preference shares
Shares which entitle the holders to a fixed rate of dividend, and the right to have any arrears paid out of future profits with priority over any distribution of profits to the holders of ordinary share capital.

current asset
Cash or other asset, e.g. stock or short term investment, held for conversion into cash in the normal course of trading.

current cost reserve
The reserve, in a current cost accounting system which includes:
(a) unrealised revaluation surpluses on fixed assets, stock and investments, and
(b) realised amounts equal to the cumulative net total of the current cost adjustments, that is,
   (i) the depreciation adjustment (and any adjustment on the disposal of fixed assets),
   (ii) the two working capital adjustments, and
   (iii) the gearing adjustment.
In general *realised* refers to an amount which has passed through the profit and loss account and *unrealised* refers to an amount which has not (SSAP 16).

current liabilities
Liabilities which fall due for payment in a relatively short period, normally less than twelve months, e.g. creditors, bank overdrafts, current taxation and dividends payable; also that part of long term loans due for repayment within one year.

debenture
The written acknowledgement of a debt by a company, usully given under its Seal, and normally containing provisions as to payment of interest and the terms of repayment of principal.
   A debenture may be secured on some or all of the assets of the company. An unsecured debenture is known as *a naked debenture.*

debtor
A person or an entity who owes money.

debtors or accounts receivable (in a balance sheet)
Money owed to the entity by customers or others.

deferred expenditure

Expenditure not charged against income in an accounting period but carried forward to be charged in the next or a subsequent period, e.g. advertising expenditure where the benefit is expected to be received in a future period.

deferred or founders' shares

A special class of shares in which the holders are not entitled to any dividend until the preference and ordinary share dividends have been paid.

Some deferred shares carry no dividend entitlement until a specified future date. These shares are usually of small nominal value and limited in number, as they attract a considerable proportion of the surplus profits after the dividend on the ordinary shares has reached a fixed rate. They are extremely valuable in a successful business.

deferred taxation

Taxation attributable to timing differences.

Timing differences are differences between profits as computed for taxation purposes and profits as stated in financial statements, which result from the inclusion of items of income and expenditure in taxation computations in periods different from those in which they are included in financial statements. Timing differences originate in one period and are capable of reversal in one or more subsequent periods. Stock appreciation relief, to the extent to which it is subject to withdrawal, comes into this category. The revaluation of an asset is regarded as creating a timing difference when it is incorporated in financial statements.

Originating timing differences are timing differences which arise in an accounting period when a transaction or event is treated differently in financial statements from the treatment accorded to the same transaction or event for taxation purposes.

Short term timing differences are originating timing differences which arise from the use of the receipts and payments basis for tax purposes and the accruals basis in financial statements. They can be identified with specific transactions and normally reverse in the next accounting period. Timing differences arise under five main categories:

(a) short term timing differences from the use of the receipts and payments basis for taxation purposes and the accruals basis in financial statements: these differences normally reverse in the next accounting period,

(b) availability of capital allowances in taxation computations which are in excess of the related depreciation charges in financial statements,
(c) availability of stock appreciation relief in taxation computations for which there is no equivalent charge in financial statements,
(d) revaluation surpluses on fixed assets for which a taxation charge does not arise until the gain is realised on disposal,
(e) surpluses on disposals of fixed assets which are subject to rollover relief (SSAP 15).

equity
Usually the issued ordinary share capital, plus attributable reserves.

equity share capital
Normally the ordinary shares of a company.

fictitious asset
An item shown as an asset in a balance sheet which has no realisable value, e.g. the preliminary and formation expenses of a company, or special advertising.

fixed asset
Any asset acquired for retention in an entity for the purpose of providing goods or services, and not held for resale in the normal course of trading.

floating charge
A general claim on the assets of an entity, given as debt security, without attachment to a specific asset.

fungible assets
Assets which are substantially indistinguishable one from another (Companies Act).

The Companies Act allows for stocks and fungible assets to be valued in the balance sheet using FIFO, or LIFO, or a weighted average price, or any other similar method. However, the use of LIFO is not currently allowed by SSAP 9.

goodwill
The intangible benefit arising from the commercial connections and reputation of a business.

When a business is purchased, any amount paid in excess of its net worth represents the value placed on the goodwill.

intangible asset
Any asset which does not have a physical identity, e.g. goodwill.

investment
Any application of money, or money's worth, which is intended to provide a return by way of interest, dividend or capital appreciation.

liabilities
The financial obligations of a business, internal (e.g. to shareholders) and external (e.g to creditors, debenture holders and, in the case of a bank loan or overdraft, to a bank).

liquid assets
Cash, and other assets readily convertible into cash, e.g. short term investments.

loan capital
Debentures and other long term loans to a business.
The holders of loan capital are paid interest but do not share in profits.

net assets
The excess of the book value of the assets of an entity over its liabilities, including loan capital.
This is equivalent to net worth.

net book value
The historical cost of an asset less any accumulated depreciation, or other provision for diminution in value, e.g. reduction to net realisable value.

net liquid funds
Cash at bank and in hand and cash equivalents, e.g. investments held as current assets, less bank overdrafts and other borrowings repayable within one year of the accounting date (SSAP 19).

net worth
The paid-up share capital and reserves.

non-voting shares
A class of share which carries no voting rights.

ordinary shares
Shares which entitle the holders to the remaining divisible profits (and, in a liquidation, the assets) after prior interests, e.g. creditors and prior charge capital, have been satisfied.

participating preference shares
Shares which usually entitle the holder to a fixed dividend, and also to participate in any surplus profits after payment of dividends at a specified rate on the ordinary shares.

payments in advance or prepayments
Expenditure on goods or services for future benefit, which is to be charged to future operations, e.g. rentals paid in advance.
These amounts are included in current assets at the end of the period in which they are incurred.

pre-acquisition profits/losses
The profits or losses of a subsidiary company, attributable to a period prior to its acquisition by a holding company, which are not available for distribution as dividends.

preference shares
Shares carrying a fixed rate of dividend, the holders of which, subject to the conditions of issue, have a prior claim to any company profits available for distribution.
Preference shareholders may also have a prior claim to the repayment of capital in the event of winding-up.

preferred creditors
Creditors entitled to full satisfaction of their claims in the event of cessation of business before other claims are met.

prior charge capital
Those classes of share and loan capital, the holders of which have a claim on the profit and assets of a business before the ordinary shareholders.

profit retained for the year
That part of profit for the financial year which is not distributed and is thus retained as revenue reserve.

provisions for liabilities and charges
Amounts retained as reasonably necessary for the purpose of providing for any liability or loss which is either likely to be incurred, or certain to be incurred but uncertain as to amount or as to the date on which it will arise (Companies Acts).

redeemable shares
Shares which are to be redeemed or are liable to be redeemed at the option of the company or the shareholder.
The redemption of such shares must comply with the provisions of section 45 of the Companies Act 1981.

reserves
Profits or surpluses which are retained in an entity.

Some entities may wish to show the division of reserves into those which are distributable and those which are not distributable under the provisions of the Companies Act (1980).

retention money or payments withheld
A sum of money representing an agreed proportion of a price for goods supplied or work completed, such proportion being withheld by the purchaser or contractee for an agreed period of time after completion, as security against failure by the supplier or contractor to fulfil his obligations under the terms of the contract.

rights issue
The raising of new capital by a company, by giving existing shareholders the right to subscribe to new shares or debentures in proportion to their current holdings.

These shares are usually issued at a discount on market price, thus reflecting the effect of the dilution of share capital. A shareholder not wishing to take up a rights issue may sell the rights on the open market.

secured creditors
Creditors whose claims are wholly or partly secured on the assets of a business.

share (in a joint stock company)
A fixed identifiable unit of capital, e.g. a share of £1 held by a member.

share capital: authorised, nominal or registered
The type, class, number and amount of the shares which a company may issue, as empowered by its memorandum of association.

share capital: called-up
The amount which the company has required shareholders to pay on the shares issued.

share capital: issued or subscribed
The type, class, number and amount of the shares held by shareholders.

share capital: paid-up
The amount which shareholders are deemed to have paid on the shares issued and called up.

share capital: uncalled
The amount of the share price of issued shares which has not been called up by the company.

share capital: unissued
The amount of the share capital authorised but not yet issued.

share option scheme
An arrangement whereby employees are given the opportunity to purchase new shares in a company at a fixed price at a future date.

share premium
The excess paid to a company by a member, either in cash or other consideration, over the nominal value of the shares issued.

sinking fund
A fund created for the redemption of a liability, or with the object of replacing an asset, by setting aside a sum periodically, and investing it (usually outside the business) so as to produce the required amount at the appropriate time.

stock (in a joint stock company)
A fixed amount of fully paid-up capital held by a stockholder any part of which can be transferred, e.g. a block of £100 of stock out of a total holding of £1,000.

tangible asset
Any asset having a physical identity, e.g. plant and machinery.

total assets
The total net book value of all assets, before deduction of any liabilities.

wasting asset
Any asset of a fixed nature which is gradually consumed or exhausted in the process of earning income, e.g. mines or quarries.

working capital
The capital available for conducting the day-to-day operations of an organisation; normally, the excess of current assets over current liabilities.

INDEX

Most items appear in this index only once, the main exceptions being concepts and variances. Items in italics appear either in a subsidiary position in the bold heading of terms or within the body of text on the page mentioned.

Printed by Libre Print, Norwich, England.